THE NATIONAL INSTITUTE OF
ECONOMIC AND SOCIAL RESEARCH

Occasional Papers
XXXIX

THE TRADE CYCLE IN BRITAIN
1958–1982

THE TRADE CYCLE
IN BRITAIN
1958–1982

ANDREW BRITTON

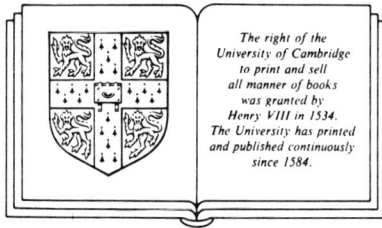

The right of the
University of Cambridge
to print and sell
all manner of books
was granted by
Henry VIII in 1534.
The University has printed
and published continuously
since 1584.

CAMBRIDGE UNIVERSITY PRESS

CAMBRIDGE
LONDON   NEW YORK   NEW ROCHELLE
MELBOURNE   SYDNEY

Published by the Press Syndicate of the University of Cambridge
The Pitt Building, Trumpington Street, Cambridge CB2 1RP
32 East 57th Street, New York, NY 10022, USA
10 Stamford Road, Oakleigh, Melbourne 3166, Australia

First published 1986

Printed in Great Britain at The Bath Press, Avon

British Library cataloguing in publication data

Britton, Andrew, *1940* –
The trade cycle in Britain 1958–1982. – (Occasional
papers/The National Institute of Economic and
Social Research; 39)
1. Business cycles – Great Britain – History –
20th century – Mathematical models
I. Title   II. National Institute of Economic and
Social Research   III. Series
338.5′42′0724   HB3783

Library of Congress cataloguing in publication data

Britton, Andrew, (Andrew J.)
The trade cycle in Britain, 1958–1982.
(Occasional papers/The National Institute of
Economic and Social Research; 39)
Bibliography: p.
Includes index.
1. Business cycles–Great Britain.   I. Title.
II. Series: Occasional papers (National Institute of
Economic and Social Research); 38.
HD3783.B77 1986   338.5′42   86–2255

ISBN 0 521 32730 X

CONTENTS

List of tables	*page*	vii
List of charts		vii
Acknowledgements		ix

1   INTRODUCTION   1

2   MATHEMATICAL MODELS OF PERIODICITY   5
Difference equations   5
Linear stochastic difference equations   7
Interactions between variables   9
More complicated mathematical models   11

3   PERIODICITY AND TRADE CYCLE THEORY   13
Seasonality   13
Examples of exogenous periodicity   15
The optimum adjustment towards equilibrium   18
Periodicity without control   21
Examples of endogenous periodicity   25
Keynesian and Marxian models of the trade cycle   27
Studying cycles in large macroeconomic models   30
The cycle and the trend   33
Conclusions   34

4   OBSERVATION AND MEASUREMENT OF PERIODICITY   36
Methodology   36
Unemployment in Britain 1851–1913   39
Unemployment in the United Kingdom and the United States
    since 1960   41
Periodicity in quarterly indicator series   45
Periodicity in unemployment and in GDP   48
Testing linearity   50
Discussion of results   52

5   EXPLAINING PERIODICITY   54
Methodology   54
Quarterly models with exogenous variables   55

6 THE HISTORY OF THE BRITISH TRADE CYCLE SINCE 1959   60
The cycle and its contemporary explanation   60
Annual models of the cycle   66
The results   70
Stocks and the cycle   75
An econometric history   77

7 SUMMARY AND DISCUSSION OF RESULTS   82

Notes   89
References   92
Index   95

TABLES

2.1 Simulations with stochastic difference equations   *page* 7
3.1 Aggregation of difference equations, some illustrative
    calculations   23
3.2 Simulations of the National Institute model   32
4.1 Unemployment in the United Kingdom, 1851–1913   40
4.2 Unemployment in the United Kingdom, 1960–81   42
4.3 Unemployment in the United States, 1960–81   43
4.4 CSO cyclical indicators: regressions without error models   46
4.5 Regressions with error models   47
4.6 Parameters implied by estimates in table 4.5   48
4.7 Autoregression model of unemployment   49
4.8 Autoregression model of GDP   51
5.1 Models with exogenous variables   57
5.2 Dynamic multipliers implied by table 5.1   58
6.1 Estimated equations using industrial production   71
6.2 Scaled residuals from estimated equations of table 6.1   72
6.3 Estimated equations for an inventory cycle   76
6.4 The path of output as explained by equation (6) of table 6.1   78
6.5 The path of output as explained by equation (8) of table 6.1   79

SYMBOLS IN THE TABLES

... not available
— nil or negligible
n.a. not applicable

CHART

1.1 The trade cycle in Britain 1958–82

ACKNOWLEDGEMENTS

I am very grateful to all those who have helped with the production of this book. First I am pleased to recognise how much it has benefited from the discussions I have had with colleagues at the National Institute, and from their comments on the work at every stage. Looking right back to the origin of some of the ideas reported here, I see that I can extend my thanks to former colleagues at the Treasury as well.

I believe the study has also benefited from the opportunities I was given to present parts of it to seminars at the London School of Economics, Birkbeck College and the Universities of Kent and Leicester. I am particularly grateful to Andrew Harvey of LSE who kindly agreed to run an estimation programme of his to obtain some of the results reported in Chapter 4. In writing this book itself I have been helped by valuable suggestions from Mike Artis and David Worswick. Naturally, responsibility for all the analysis and conclusions rests with me alone.

It is not easy to combine econometric work with management tasks. Little progress could have been made without the support of a research assistant, first Judith Payne and then Martin Wall. My thanks go also to my secretary, Ann Wright, and to Frances Robinson who prepared the text for publication.

I would also like to take this opportunity of expressing my thanks to all the financial supporters of the Institute and especially to the Economic and Social Research Council which provided funds specifically for the work reported here.

AJCB
November 1985

INTRODUCTION

The subject matter of this study is best described by reference to a chart. Its starting point is the visual impression made by the series plotted in chart 1.1. The human eye is notoriously prone to see patterns where none exist, to see faces in the flames or omens in the flight of birds. Even if that temptation is recognised, however, it is difficult to resist some pattern recognition here. One series is a composite indicator devised to illustrate cyclical chronology. The other is based on a survey of manufacturing industry. Surely the time paths of both these series show a systematic tendency to repeat themselves at intervals of about five years. The main purpose of this study is to examine this phenomenon, explore some possible explanations and to discover how systematic this apparent periodicity actually is. Is it the same in the 1970s as in the 1960s? Would it be sensible to extrapolate it into the future? The two series plotted

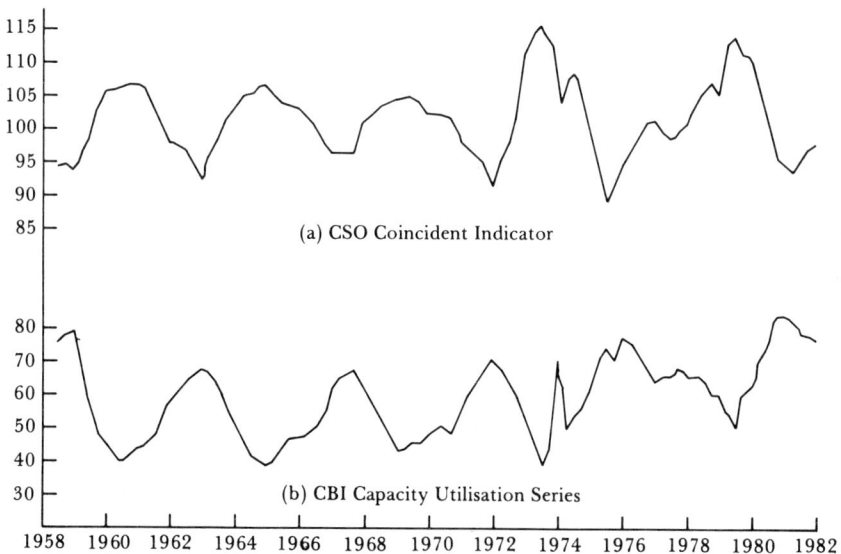

Chart 1.1. The trade cycle in Britain 1958–82
Source: *Economic Trends.*

have been chosen from the many available because they illustrate this apparent periodicity rather well. They do so because they are not subject to much short-term or erratic variation from month to month and because neither has a rising or falling trend to confuse the cyclical pattern. The phenomenon, however, is a pervasive one in the economy and some trade-cycle behaviour can be observed in almost all the indicators commonly used to monitor the behaviour of the economy.

The first series is one deliberately constructed by the Central Statistical Office (CSO) to identify the phases of the economic cycle.[1] It is a composite based on a whole range of indicators; it has been smoothed to reduce short-term fluctuation and detrended by reference to a five-year moving average. These prior adjustments must be borne in mind when using this series as evidence about the character of the cycle, but it would be quite wrong to conclude that the periodicity is simply an illusion resulting from them. Similar procedures applied to American data for example, also produce a smooth, trend-free series with a limited number of clearly defined turning points. In the American data, however, the gaps between turning points are not even roughly the same length from cycle to cycle.

The second series comes from the Confederation of British Industry's (CBI) survey and records the percentage of respondents who say they have spare production capacity. This series is plotted here with no 'doctoring' or prior adjustment at all.[2] It happens to be a relatively smooth and trend-free indicator, and therefore illustrates the periodic character of the cycle almost as clearly as the CSO's artificial construct.

To avoid any possible ambiguity at the outset, periodicity, which is the main focus of this study, should be distinguished from persistence, which is the focus of much recent writing about the trade cycle, or the business cycle as Americans call it. (The term 'cyclicality' is often used loosely to mean either periodicity or persistence.) Persistence is the tendency of the economy when disturbed from some supposed equilibrium position to move back gradually rather than jump back at once. Persistence determines the duration of cyclical fluctuations, and hence the predictability of economic conditions from one year to the next. Periodicity can be seen as a special case of persistence and must give rise to some degree of predictability. One could say that the average length of a cycle is a question of persistence but the variability of cycle lengths is a question of periodicity. To avoid confusion I shall always use the word 'periodicity' to describe fluctuations which tend to be of constant length, since 'cyclicality' is nowadays often used of variables which show some persistence but which are not periodic at all.[3]

There is a rich literature concerned with periodicity starting in the nineteenth century and extending up to about the end of the 1950s.[4]

A very useful account of the state of knowledge and theory at that time is given in *The Trade Cycle* by R. C. O. Matthews, published in 1959. The striking fact is that all the data shown on the chart describe history since that book was written and since, in fact, interest in periodicity amongst economists in general has waned. It would appear that any economist who had read the literature on the subject, up to and including Matthews' book, and on that basis predicted periodic behaviour in the next quarter of a century, would have been rather impressively vindicated by events.

Although theorists anticipated the periodicity with which this study is concerned, it is necessary to reconsider several theoretical issues before making a closer examination of the data. Trade-cycle theory has not stood still since the late 1950s, although very little attention has been given to periodicity. This study, therefore, includes a modest attempt at re-examining periodicity and its place in trade-cycle theory as it is today.

The focus of this study is periodicity. No attempt will be made to review the vast literature on the trade cycle, of which only a small and decreasing sub-set deals with periodicity at all. A comprehensive and up-to-date survey article will be found in Zarnowitz (1985). The position taken in that article on the issue of periodicity is of some interest since it provides such an authoritative introduction to the business cycle literature. The section of the article on the 'stylised facts' begins: 'The term "business cycle" is a misnomer insofar as no unique periodicities are involved.' Yet further down the same page we read, 'The individual phase and cycle durations show considerable variability over time ... However, when the relatively rare outliers are discounted, fairly clear central tendencies emerge. Thus the ranges $1\frac{1}{2}$ to 3 years, 1 to 2 years and $2\frac{1}{2}$ to 5 years account for three fourths or more of the peacetime expansions, contractions and full cycles in the United States, respectively.' This 'central tendency', which is more marked in the United Kingdom than in the United States, is another way of describing the phenomenon with which the present study is concerned. Despite the passage just quoted it has received little or no analysis in the recent literature to which Zarnowitz refers.

The remainder of this book falls into four main parts. Chapter 2 gives an elementary account of the mathematics of periodicity, aimed at the general economist reader. Chapter 3, which is also intended to be access-ible rather than rigorous, contains some ideas about how periodicity might fit into contemporary trade-cycle theory. Chapter 4 examines a variety of ways in which statistical analysis can describe the time series and their periodicity. It is concerned mainly with the last twenty-five years in Britain but it also makes some brief historical and cross-country comparisons. Chapter 5 is more ambitious because it seeks to explain the periodicity of British data since the late 1950s by building models that have some behavioural content. These four parts are followed in Chapter 6 by a year-by-year account of the trade cycle based on contemporary reporting, brought together with a statistical analysis of the data as we now have them. The result is an 'econometric history' of the twenty-five year period. The chronology of the trade cycle is explained in part by a succession of external events, in part by a tendency to periodicity, which seems to be inherent to the behaviour of the economy itself or to the way in which economic policy has been conducted.

2

MATHEMATICAL MODELS OF PERIODICITY

DIFFERENCE EQUATIONS

The main aim of this study is to give an economic or behavioural account of periodicity. The mathematics is a step in that direction and not an end in itself.[1] It is helpful in establishing different categories of periodic behaviour and in suggesting the forms of interaction from which it could arise.

The best starting point is a second-order linear difference equation

$$y = ay_{-1} + by_{-2}$$

The time path of y following this equation will be periodic if the roots of the equation

$$1 - aL - bL^2 = 0$$

are complex. In other words, if those roots are complex, any perturbation of y away from its equilibrium value (zero in this case) will result in an oscillating path through positive and negative values, which persistently overshoots the equilibrium. If the second coefficient b is greater than unity in absolute value, then the oscillations will be explosive, increasing indefinitely in amplitude. If that coefficient is less than unity in absolute value, then the oscillations will damp down over time and y will stay closer and closer to its equilibrium value.

This equation is just a starting point because periodicity does not typically involve cycles which either die away or explode. This objection can be removed in two quite different ways. The first starts from a stable damped system and adds a random disturbance term which is continually applying new shocks to the system and so keeping it in oscillation. The second starts from an unstable or explosive system and adds non-linearities which keep the amplitude of the resulting fluctuations within bounds. Both approaches were well developed in the trade cycle literature by the 1950s.

In this study we shall be concerned mainly with the linear stochastic model, that is, the one with random disturbances applied to a system with a stable equilibrium. This strategic choice may require some justification, since the non-linear alternative has a most impressive intellectual pedigree and important work is still being done today within that tradition.[2]

The first justification is that the economy surely is stochastic. It is subject to a large number of individually small influences which are not predictable by economics or indeed by any kind of science. The examples usually quoted are labour disputes, foreign wars and general elections, but in fact any event (or rumour of an event) which could disturb (or be thought to disturb) the economy from its theoretical equilibrium will do. What is involved are events which are individually small, not major crises such as the second world war or even the OPEC oil price increases. All econometrics is conducted on the assumption that there is background noise of this kind (as well as some apparent noise caused by measurement error). In any case, if we believe that the world is stochastic, there is no need to resort to non-linearity to explain why oscillations persist.

The non-linear alternative, moreover, is so successful in explaining periodicity that it is not well equipped to explain why periodicity occurs in some economies but not others, or to a greater or lesser extent in one economy as compared with another. The non-linear model is explosive or unstable in the neighbourhood of its equilibrium although it is globally stable and cannot diverge from that equilibrium indefinitely. The path of a variable defined by such a system would follow a limit cycle moving backwards and forwards between a floor and a ceiling with monotonous regularity. Actual economies do not behave like that. Therefore the non-linear model itself must be made stochastic if it is to fit the real world. Indeed, if one is to explain why some cycles fail to reach the floor or the ceiling, and why some cycles are quite a lot longer or shorter than others, the limit cycle model is not the obvious choice of mathematical representation. Needless to say one could explain all irregularities if the characteristics of the model itself, and hence the positions of the floor and the ceiling, and the frequency of oscillation, were allowed to shift randomly from time to time. That, however, would be to abandon the whole object of the exercise, which is to find a stable (in the sense of unchanging) mathematical structure which describes the periodicity we observe.[3]

We need not, however, on the basis of these informal arguments, abandon the idea of the limit cycle altogether. As we shall see in the next section, one very interesting mathematical model is a second-order difference equation close to the borderline of stability, where the second coefficient, b in the notation used above, is close to unity. We can even leave open the question whether that coefficient is a little below or a little above unity and whether it is strictly independent of the position, relative to equilibrium, of the variable whose behaviour the equation describes. These alternatives can, as a later section shows, be tested empirically.

LINEAR STOCHASTIC DIFFERENCE EQUATIONS

It may not be immediately obvious intuitively that random shocks applied to a system can result in regular periodicity.[4] After all, each individual random shock will produce its own damped oscillation in response and it is not obvious that a coherent or visible regularity will result from a sequence of such responses if they are initiated at random. Intuition is not at fault here, for it is only if the system is quite close to instability that periodicity will be visible to the naked eye.

One way of demonstrating this is by simulation, that is, by repeated calculations (on a computer) to create artificial data. Table 2.1 illustrates

Table 2.1. *Simulations with stochastic difference equations*

Equations

(1) $y = 1.745y_{-1} - 1.0y_{-2} + u$	(2) $y = 1.7y_{-1} - 0.95y_{-2} + u$
(3) $y = 1.655y_{-1} - 0.9y_{-2} + u$	(4) $y = 1.608y_{-1} - 0.85y_{-2} + u$
(5) $y = 1.56y_{-1} - 0.8y_{-2} + u$	(6) $y = 1.51y_{-1} - 0.75y_{-2} + u$
(7) $y = 1.459y_{-1} - 0.7y_{-2} + u$	(8) $y = 1.406y_{-1} - 0.65y_{-2} + u$

Number of half cycles

Time period	(1)	(2)	(3)	(4)	(5)	(6)	(7)	(8)
1	1	0	9	7	9	10	26	25
2	2	2	8	6	13	11	21	18
3	2	5	10	14	11	19	16	13
4	6	6	16	21	15	22	20	20
5	20	24	35	27	23	20	25	32
6	94	62	61	23	26	21	21	19
7	36	37	24	36	22	12	16	19
8	2	12	13	10	16	11	7	8
9	1	1	6	10	8	2	11	4
10	2	0	1	1	7	9	7	6
11	0	0	0	5	6	3	3	8
12	0	3	0	1	4	7	2	2
>12	0	4	0	5	4	13	10	10

Note: Run for 1000 time periods in each case.

the results of one such exercise. The procedure was as follows: a second-order linear difference equation with a stochastic error term was programmed and a thousand successive replications were calculated. The programme recognised points at which the solution path crossed zero and counted the number of time periods since the preceding such cross-over point. This is defined as a half cycle and the distribution of half-cycle lengths for the complete run of a thousand time periods was tabulated. This analysis of the artificial data has something in common with visual inspection. Cross-over points are used to define the cycle rather than turning points because the latter may just be local maxima or minima which the eye would dismiss as aberrations.

The results are tabulated for eight different equations all of which have the same underlying cyclical frequency (dependent on the roots of the corresponding quadratic equations) and this implies a half cycle of just over six time periods. The equations differ only in damping: equation (1) is right on the borderline between stability and instability, then damping increases in each successive equation. As the tabulations show, the borderline case gives a very regular periodicity with almost all the half cycles between five and seven time periods in length. As the damping or stability is increased the regularity is decreased. By equation (5), in which the second coefficient has fallen to 0.8, it is doubtful whether the naked eye would spot the periodicity at all. In a sense periodicity exists so long as the underlying equation has complex roots, but in the present study it is visible periodicity of the kind shown by the chart in Chapter 1 which is of most interest. This disappears about halfway across the table. (In this particular example it disappears at a value of about 0.8 for the second coefficient of the equation. But this observation cannot be generalised since the damping effect should be measured relative to the number of time periods per half cycle. For example, the critical range for that coefficient would be different for monthly, quarterly or annual observations of the same data series.)

These simulations may help to make an important, and not intuitively obvious, point. A more rigorous demonstration is possible. This could in principle be done by reference to the analytical distribution of half cycles[5] but this would involve some quite intractable mathematics. A simpler approach is to look at autocorrelations.[6]

If a variable y follows a path described by the equation

$$y = ay_{-1} + by_{-2} + u$$

where u is a 'white noise' disturbance term, then

$$E(yy_{-1}) = aE(y_{-1}^2) + bE(y_{-1}y_{-2})$$

or, more generally, if $r(N)$ is the correlation between values of y separated from each other by N time periods,

$$r(N) = ar(N-1) + br(N-2)$$

But this is itself a second-order difference equation in N which has the same roots as the equation in $y(t)$ from which it is derived. Suppose therefore that the equation in $y(t)$ has complex roots implying a specific period of oscillation and a specific degree of damping. The series of autocorrelations will have the same period and the same degree of damping. Thus, as one would expect, the autocorrelation between observations separated by a half-cycle length will be negative, whilst that between observations at a full-cycle length will be positive. Moreover, the autocorrelations at one-and-a-half-cycle lengths will be negative, at two-cycle lengths positive, and so on. The damping determines how rapidly the correlations fall away towards zero. If they fall away slowly (when the coefficient b is close to unity) the correlation at the first cyclical peak will be high and the cycles relatively easy to see with the 'naked eye'. If the correlations fall away rapidly (and b is close to zero) then the periodicity of the series will be obscured.

Thus a stochastic linear second-order difference equation is a very useful mathematical model for exploring periodicity. According to the values of its two parameters it can generate at one extreme very regular periodicity, at the other no periodicity at all. It can also explain periodicity which is quite regular, but nevertheless subject to some variations in amplitude or frequency. Thus it seems appropriate as a model of the degree of periodicity we observe in recent British data, whilst at the same time explaining why it is that in some economies and some periods of history, which do not differ fundamentally from that data source, periodicity does not seem to occur at all. Much use will be made of it in this study.

INTERACTIONS BETWEEN VARIABLES

Trade-cycle behaviour is pervasive. This is to say it is common to a very large number of economic indicators, dominating ther behaviour of some and discernible in the behaviour of most. If these common fluctuations are periodic then all the variables involved (output, employment, spending, prices and so on) will share the same frequency and damping or regularity in their cyclical behaviour. They will, however, differ from one another in phase (some variables leading, others lagging) and in the amplitude of their fluctuations.

Such common behaviour could arise because one variable influences another. For example, the cycle in employment is often thought to result from the cycle in output, which it generally follows with a short lag. Alternatively, the cycle in all the variables we observe could arise because they are all subject to a common influence originating outside the economy altogether. For example, British output, employment, prices and all other British variables could pick up their cyclical pattern from the behaviour of the world economy. One could then say that the British cycle is due to exogenous influences and, in engineering terms, describe it as a 'forced' oscillation.

Oscillations may be 'forced' by variables we can measure, like world trade and output, or by variables we cannot measure or even identify.

In the latter case we would find that the best mathematical model would be one in which periodicity arose from the behaviour of the error term itself. Clearly this would be a difficult kind of periodicity to explain in terms of economics as opposed to mathematics but it is a logical possibility that cannot be excluded.

Perhaps the most interesting case to explore is the one where periodicity arises from an interaction between two or more variables which can actually be observed. In the simplest example of this type of system two first-order difference equations interact to produce a second-order dynamic system.

For example

$$x = ax_{-1} + by_{-1} + u \tag{1a}$$
$$y = cy_{-1} + dx_{-1} + v \tag{1b}$$

and therefore

$$x = (a+c)x_{-1} - (ac-bd)x_{-2} + u - cu_{-1} + bv_{-1} \tag{2a}$$

and

$$y = (a+c)y_{-1} - (ac-bd)y_{-2} + v - av_{-1} + du_{-1} \tag{2b}$$

The second-order difference equations describing the behaviour of x and y have the same coefficients. Therefore, if those coefficients imply periodicity (for which it is necessary that either b or d is negative), then x and y will have the same frequency and damping, but differ in phase and amplitude. The error term in the derived equations will not be 'white noise'. If the errors in the original first-order equations are 'white' then these derived errors will be first-order moving average errors. They cannot produce 'forced' periodicity, but any kind of error autocorrelation affects the properties of the system and makes statistical estimation more complicated.

An interaction model of this kind has been used by biologists to explain the periodicity observed in animal populations.[7] In that application x might be the number of predators which increases at a rate dependent on y the number of prey. Conversely, with the parameter d negative, the increase in the numbers of prey is reduced by the population of predators. As we shall see, there are many different ways in which this mathematical idea could be applied to relations amongst economic variables.

One special case of this kind of interaction deserves special mention. Suppose that the coefficient c in equation (1b) is equal to unity. This implies that there is a relationship between the level of y and the integral or summation of x. (Indeed if the error term v were omitted, y could actually *be* the summation of x.) That being so equation (1a) could be interpreted as an 'integral control mechanism', because the behaviour of the variable x depends not only on its value in the preceding period but also on the whole past history of its behaviour as summarised by integration. If the 'feedback' from that integral is negative, then periodicity may possibly (but not necessarily) result. Such mechanisms are a familiar idea in control engineering and have many applications or analogies in economics.

MORE COMPLICATED MATHEMATICAL MODELS

Periodicity can, as we have seen, be the result of quite simple interactions. The economy, however, is an extremely complicated system which involves, strictly speaking, the interaction of millions of variables. Even econometric models which are concerned only with the interaction of some of the more important macroeconomic aggregates can contain hundreds or even thousands of variables. Is it possible that such rich variety of behaviour can really be summarised by one second-order difference equation or two first-order difference equations interacting?

As a concession to realism perhaps we should imagine the economy as described not by a second-order difference equation but by a very high-order difference equation, say one-hundredth order. Despite its great length and the rich variety of the possible behaviour such a system may describe, a one-hundredth order equation may in practice be dominated by the behaviour of its least stable root. Periodicity that is sufficiently regular to be visible to the 'naked eye' can occur only if there is a pair of complex roots which is not subject to much damping. It is relatively unlikely that even one root pair of this kind will occur in the appropriate frequency band even in a very high-order difference equation. It is quite possible therefore that just one such pair of roots exists in an equation even of the hundredth order. The autocorrelation function of such a one-hundredth order difference equation may look very like that of a second-order equation.

A related point can be made in the context of the prey and predators model. Instead of one kind of prey and one kind of predator it may be more realistic to imagine a variety of carnivorous species and a variety of herbivores. Their interactions may be very complicated and involve many different rates of population increase and inter-dependency. Nevertheless, the outcome could be just one cycle involving all species. This must be the case if there are only three species, since a third-order system can have only one pair of complex roots. It could well be the result even if there are many species, especially if all prey and predator species reproduce at broadly the same rate.

Having said this, it must also be recognised that a generalisation of the second-order difference equations we have been considering may sometimes involve not one cycle but many. This would not be altogether out of keeping with trade-cycle theory which has on occasion distinguished more than one cycle in economic data (a housing cycle for example superimposed on an industrial investment cycle, not to mention short inventory cycles or long waves). We have also to recognise that cycles of different length and regularity may be generated in different countries but transmitted internationally by trade or capital movements.

It is, moreover, theoretically possible that a high-order difference equation might, by pure chance, happen to involve more than one complex root pair having much the same frequency. This would enhance the 'visibility' of the resulting periodicity, even if the roots individually were heavily damped.[8]

Such possibilities must be mentioned for completeness, but one must also bear in mind that we are embarking on a study of periodicity in one country over a period of about twenty-five years, and the length of a typical cycle is of the order of five years. This puts a high premium on parsimony in the design of mathematical models. If the truth which we are seeking is very complicated then we know our quest will be in vain. If, however, a simple explanation seems to suffice then we know that for the present we will do no better however hard we try.

3

PERIODICITY AND TRADE-CYCLE THEORY

The literature in journals, articles and books from the 1920s to the 1960s abounds with theoretical models of the trade cycle which purport to explain periodicity. Within the framework of a second-order linear difference equation it is not difficult to multiply theoretically plausible models based on the interaction of two or more variables. The aim of this section is not to catalogue such theories or to invent new ones but rather to relate the concept of periodicity to relatively new developments in macroeconomics. Is periodicity compatible with 'rational' expectations? Could it be the result of optimising behaviour by all economic agents? Such questions have scarcely been addressed in the recent literature of business-cycle theory which is concerned rather to explain how any fluctuations can persist. A complete, formal, integration of periodicity with that literature is beyond the scope of this study. Nevertheless, a brief, and relatively informal, exploration of the issues may be rewarding.

It could be said that there is no need to explore the implications of rational expectations for the periodicity of trade cycles because the very existence of periodicity is in doubt. Why ask whether periodicity is compatible with rational expectations, since if the British economy really does behave in a periodic way then the expectations of the large number of agents who are, at least prior to this study, ignorant of that fact cannot be rational? The point is well made, but it does not eliminate the need for theoretical consideration of this kind. It may be that many decision takers are at least dimly aware of the sort of patterns suggested by the indicator series we have used to illustrate periodicity. They may have absorbed from experience, even unconsciously, the idea that 'stop' always follows 'go', that each boom leads to a slump, that 'what goes up must come down'. Moreover, even if no trace of such ideas were evident at the present time, one must suppose, if periodicity is indeed systematic, that the message will eventually be read and understood. Perhaps twenty-five years is just not long enough. In that case it is certainly interesting to ask whether periodicity could continue despite that discovery or whether it is one of those phenomena for which discovery spells extinction.

SEASONALITY

An obvious and pervasive cycle, of very regular periodicity, seldom discussed in the context of business cycle theory, is seasonality. Its most important characteristic for present purposes is its predictability. The timing of the seasons is known with certainty and their effect on economic activity and prices is well documented and understood. Seasonality will therefore serve very well as an illustration of some of the characteristics to be expected of a trade cycle under rational expectations. Indeed models of the trade cycle under rational expectations are much more believable as realistic descriptions of seasonality than as realistic descriptions of the trade cycle!

In the absence of storage costs, a 'perfect' market would eliminate all seasonal variation in prices, since any such variation would offer costless risk-free profits to arbitrageurs. Such arbitrage can indeed be seen in operation in financial markets and statisticians do not find it necessary to 'seasonally adjust' interest rates or exchange rates. There are other prices, however, which do vary systematically through the year, because the goods in question are perishable, too costly to store, or for some other reason not sufficiently marketable for perfect arbitrage to develop. Aggregate price indices, such as the retail price index, show marked seasonal variations. Predictable cyclical price behaviour could occur under rational expectations for those kinds of goods and for aggregate price indices but not, it would seem, for exchange rates or relative interest rates. The last observation needs some qualification, however, if the cycle length is significant and price variation substantial over the cycle. Strictly, all one can say is that no risk-free gains in real purchasing power could be secured by systematically buying and selling financial assets at different points in the predictable cycle.

Output levels also vary with the seasons in response to predictable rhythms both of supply and of demand. Since the purpose of this discussion is to draw analogies with the trade cycle, which is by common consent the result of variation in demand, we may pass over the interesting questions raised by predictable variation in supply. Firms facing predictable variations in demand, reflected in prices or in the length of their order books, may choose to vary output less than in proportion. It is generally accepted that there are, in most activities, costs associated with changing the level of production. The variations in demand will therefore sometimes be matched by variations in stock levels as well as variations in output. (Production of Christmas cards would serve as a rather extreme example.) Employment may well vary even less than output over the year because of the costs of hiring or firing. In some occupations, however, part-year work is a well established convention, providing a good example of 'equilibrium' unemployment which could also exist in the recession phase of a fully predictable trade cycle.

The capital stock may not vary at all perceptibly with the seasons because the costs of adjustment in response to variations in output over a relatively short time scale must usually be prohibitive. In a theoretical model, however, if not in the real world, there is a place for a seasonal 'accelerator' which would tend to increase the amplitude of seasonal variation. At an aggregate level there would also be traces of a seasonal 'multiplier', but if we assume that seasonal variation in income is predictable, then it would be mainly, if not entirely, offset by variation in savings or in borrowing.

That is as far as the discussion of seasonality need be taken in the present context, although it may be of sufficient interest in its own right to merit more extensive treatment. Two conclusions are worth special emphasis. The first is a straightforward matter of timing. There is no reason for one variable to lag behind another when all are moving in response to a predictable cycle. Even when adjustment costs are important there is no reason to delay adjustment when it is known that adjustment will have to take place.

The second is more fundamental. Seasonal variation has been described in a way consistent with 'continuous equilibrium', that is, with market clearing all the year round. That does seem generally appropriate in a model of seasonality, but even here there are exceptions. Prices do not always vary enough to prevent some systematic alternation of excess and deficient demand in summer and winter. Hotel rooms, rail fares, theatre tickets, seem to provide examples of prices which show some seasonal variation but not enough to eliminate excess or deficient demand. Most important, however, is the almost complete absence of seasonal variation in wage rates. That may indicate, despite what was said earlier, that much of the seasonal variation in unemployment is of a 'disequilibrium' kind. That, too, would have implications for our understanding of the trade cycle.

EXAMPLES OF EXOGENOUS PERIODICITY

Seasonality is exogenous. If it is to provide a close analogue for the trade cycle then we should look for an exogenous source for fluctuations in the British economy having a frequency in the region of five years throughout the period since the late 1950s. This search will be continued in the statistical investigation of later sections. Here it is necessary only to clarify the logical implications of some possible explanations of this kind.

At one time it was thought that periodicity in economic data, especially perhaps in price data, could be accounted for by periodicity in the weather and hence in the productivity of agriculture. That periodicity was, in turn, supposed by some writers to be related to sunspots. Fortunately perhaps it is not necessary here to go into the theoretical basis for this claim or the statistical methods used to defend it. The trade cycle with which we are concerned here is a phenomenon chiefly of the manufacturing and construction sectors of the economy, not of agriculture.

A much more plausible explanation for the British trade cycle, widely believed, is that it is caused by fluctuations in the instruments of demand management, fiscal and monetary policy. This hypothesis will be discussed at some length later in this book. Here we need only draw a rather important distinction. We must distinguish the view that such policy measures are exogenous from the view that they are endogenous. Very broadly speaking the first view seems to predominate in America, the second in this country.

Exogenous policy in this context means policy which is not significantly influenced by the state of the trade cycle itself. The view of some 'new classical' monetarists, for example, is that the American business cycle results from unpredictable changes in the monetary growth rate resulting in 'shocks' which produce a certain degree of 'persistence'.[1,2] (The emphasis here is on the word 'unpredictable'. Predictable changes are discussed below.) If policy changes were endogenous, that is to say systematic responses to, for example, the level of output or the rate of inflation, then they would not be 'shocks' at all. Unpredictable policy is necessarily exogenous. Moreover, unpredictable policy changes, even if they produce persistence, cannot be the origin of periodicity. This follows from the observation that periodicity is, of its nature, at least to a degree predictable. It would be a contradiction to speak of 'periodic shocks'. The shocks in question are supposed to be 'innovations' in the statistical sense, that is, events which could not be predicted from the past behaviour of the variable in question.

The proposition that monetary policy has no effect at all on output if it is predictable should probably be treated as a limiting case. If the extreme 'new classical' assumptions required for this result are relaxed, then even predictable monetary policy changes have some, albeit transitory, real effects. Moreover, even in the most 'new classical' of worlds other instruments of demand management, including fiscal policy changes, will influence the level of economic activity (if not always in the way the authorities intended). Thus, either by generalising the description of economic policy or by relaxing the assumptions about the 'neutrality of money', one can justify the view that policy is the cause of economic fluctuations, even though it is to some extent predictable, for example periodic. In other words, a theoretical case can be made out for a periodic 'political business cycle'.[3]

Again one must distinguish exogenous policy from endogenous policy. For the moment our concern is only with the former. Why, in that case, one might ask, should policy be periodic? A natural answer, at least to an American, would be that presidential elections occur just as regularly as the seasons of the year and occur moreover at what are commonly called 'business-cycle frequencies', that is to say every fourth year. The argument, put rather brutally, is that the level of output is manipulated by the authorities to produce a brief period of prosperity as the election approaches, with the consequent downturn coming after the votes have been cast. (The electorate in this simple model do not understand what is going on.)

Since the maximum lifetime of a Parliament in Britain is five years, this may seem an appealing explanation of periodicity here as well. It must be conceded, however, that this is a maximum life, not, as in America, a fixed and invariable life. Elections in this country took place in 1959, 1964, 1966, 1970, 1974 (twice), 1979, and 1983. Thus the regularity of the electoral cycle was broken in the mid-1960s and again, less seriously, in the mid-1970s. At any time the date of the next election is a matter of speculation, not of certainty. This is not to deny that electoral considerations have influenced economic policy in this country, although they may not, as we shall see, have influenced policy in a consistent way. In this country, unlike America, it is also possible that the state of the economy and the phase of the trade cycle may influence the timing of elections as well as *vice versa*. This requires an extension of the theory of the 'political business cycle' which will not detain us here. The main point to make is that the electoral cycle here is very different from seasonality. It is neither exogenous nor predictable.

For completeness one should mention the possibility that apparently cyclical movements could be caused by the alternations of Labour and Conservative governments pursuing different economic strategies or having different priorities amongst economic objectives. A political cycle could cause an economic cycle. Whatever the theoretical interest of an interdisciplinary model of this kind it does not fit the facts for the period of this study even approximately. Labour and Conservative governments have presided over both expansionary and contractionary phases of the cycle.

This brief account of 'political business cycle' theory suggests that the most interesting hypotheses of this kind will be those properly classified under 'endogenous periodicity' rather than 'exogenous'. These will be discussed below. It remains in this section to mention the one other source of exogenous periodicity which will play a major role in our discussion of recent periodicity in Britain.

The British economy is very open to influences from abroad. These include the effect of world trade on our exports, of world inflation on our inflation rate, world interest rates on our interest rates and our exchange rate, world prices for raw materials and food on our costs, and so on. Undoubtedly some of the fluctuations in the British economy are imported. It is possible that the periodicity we observe may be imported as well. Should this be the case one might not wish to end the study with that finding but rather to explore the underlying reasons for periodicity in the world economy. Some of the hypotheses that would suggest themselves might be of broadly the same kind as those which we shall be considering in a British context. There would nevertheless be differences. In studying the British economy in isolation one can take the price of most raw materials as given; for the world economy as a whole they could be a major cause of cyclical fluctuations. Conversely, economic policy would play a more important part in the discussion of economic fluctuations in a single economy than in the world as a whole.

Within the British economy the trade cycle is pervasive, in the sense that it is perceptible in all regions and most industries. Output, employment and prices throughout the economy move together, or follow each other with a well established pattern of leads and lags, although of course each industry and, to a lesser extent, each region has its own peculiar fluctuations superimposed on the national pattern. If the world economy were integrated to the same extent as a national economy it would no longer be meaningful to distinguish the cyclical behaviour of each country. That is not the case now, or in the period of history to be discussed in this study, although it may well be the direction in which we are moving.

THE OPTIMUM ADJUSTMENT TOWARDS EQUILIBRIUM

Could periodicity arise from deliberate and well informed decisions, or is it an indication of some kind of irrationality or market imperfection? We are now turning attention from theoretical models in which periodicity is exogenous to models in which it is endogenous. In the pre-1960 literature of trade-cycle theory the reasons for lagged adjustment were perhaps not spelt out as clearly as would be expected today. More generally the foundations of macroeconomic cycles in microeconomic decision taking have become a central concern of economic theory in a way they were not a generation ago.

In this section we shall consider the behaviour of a single economic agent, typically a producer, and the circumstances in which his behaviour, typically the level of output produced, may be periodic. In the next section we shall consider how behaviour by two or more agents, or groups of agents, could interact to produce periodicity. In both sections it will be necessary to introduce some more mathematics.[4]

The first case to consider is the relatively familiar one of the agent who faces both costs of adjustment and costs of departing from equilibrium. In this case periodicity cannot arise from optimal behaviour, since it will never be advantageous to overshoot equilibrium.

The agent's objective can be expressed as the minimisation over all future time periods of the cost function

$$\Sigma[(x - x^*)^2 + \lambda(x - x_{-1})^2] \tag{1}$$

where x is the variable under his control and x^* is its static equilibrium. For simplicity any discounting of the future has been ignored and costs have been approximated as quadratic.

This function can be minimised with respect to x (bearing in mind that this involves costs incurred in the next time period as well as the current one).

$$(x - x^*) + \lambda(x - x_{-1}) - \lambda(x_{+1} - x) = 0 \tag{2}$$

where x_{+1} is the planned future value of x.
To turn it into an operational decision rule it is necessary to eliminate the future value of x from the equation and replace it by a term reflecting expectations about x^* (the equilibrium value of x) in all future time periods. This solution is best expressed using an operator notation where L indicates a lag of one period and L^{-1} indicates a lead. Equation (2) can be rewritten as:

$$(x - x^*) + \lambda(1 - L)x - \lambda(L^{-1} - 1)x = 0$$

or

$$[-\lambda L^{-1} + (1 + 2\lambda) - \lambda L]x = x^*$$

This can be rearranged so that only the lag operator, and not the lead, appears on the left hand side.

$$(1 - aL)x = [2 - (a + 1/a)/(L^{-1} - 1/a)]x^* \tag{3}$$

where a is defined by $a + 1/a \equiv (2 + 1/\lambda)$
Since only a first-order difference equation in x is involved there can be no question of periodicity or even overshooting unless x^* itself is an endogenous variable. Costs of adjustment on their own do not explain periodicity.

Suppose, however, that there are also costs associated with cumulated deviations from equilibrium, for example because these will lead to an inappropriately high or low level of stocks or orders in hand. Now there would be some rationale for overshooting or periodicity. For example, the need to restore stocks to an appropriate level after a period of under- or over-production can readily suggest overshooting in both directions. This can be confirmed algebraically.

The objective to be minimised in (1) can be replaced by:

$$\Sigma[(x - x^*)^2 + \lambda(x - x_{-1})^2 + \mu(S - S^*)^2] \tag{1a}$$

where $S = (\nu S_{-1}) + x$

The minimum cost solution is now given by

$$(x - x^*) + \lambda(x - x_{-1}) - \lambda(x_{+1} - x) = \theta \tag{2a}$$

and

$$\mu(S - S^*) = \nu\theta_{+1} - \theta \tag{2b}$$

where θ is a 'shadow price' which has been introduced as an extra variable simply for ease of exposition.

This gives rise to two simultaneous equations in x and θ using lag and lead operators:

$$(1 - aL)(L^{-1} - 1/a)x = -1/\lambda \, (\theta + x^*) \tag{3a}$$
$$(1 - \nu L)(L^{-1} - 1/\nu)\theta = \mu/\nu \, [x - (1 - \nu L)S^*] \tag{3b}$$

Combining these two equations must result in a second-order equation in lagged values of x as well as a 'forward-looking' second-order term in expectations about the equilibrium values x^* and S^*.

$$[(1 - aL)(1 - \nu L)(L^{-1} - 1/a)(L^{-1} - 1/\nu) + 1/\lambda \, \mu/\nu]x = A \tag{3c}$$

where A is exogenous to this decision and depends on current, past and future values of x^* and S^*.

The rather forbidding expression inside the square brackets involves both leads and lags. To understand its implications for the behaviour of x it must be factorised into two separate polynomials, one in the lag operator and one in the lead operator. This parallels the derivation of equation (3) above.

The key to this factorisation is symmetry. If the expression in square brackets is expanded it will be seen that the coefficients on the leads and the lags are identical, as they were in the derivation of equation (3). The form of the factorisation must therefore be a generalisation of equation (3).

$$(1 - \alpha L + \beta L^2)x = A/(L^{-2}\frac{\alpha}{\beta} \, L^{-1} + 1/\beta) \tag{4}$$

The behaviour of x will be periodic if the roots of the second-order polynomial in the lag operator applied to it are complex. It is not possible too give any simple or intuitive account of the circumstances in which this condition will be realised. It depends on the values of all the parameters involved. Periodicity is a possible outcome, but not inevitable. If it does occur, the frequency and damping (or regularity) of the cycles must also depend on all the parameters in the optimisation problem (that is on λ, μ and ν).

The significance of this result for trade-cycle theory is twofold. First one could make a normative point. Periodic trade cycles are not necessarily undesirable. They could be the socially optimum behaviour of the economy in response to 'stochastic' shocks of the kind we have described. This means that counter-cyclical policy might be misconceived. In saying that one must bear in mind that we are concerned here with cycles that are symmetrical about the equilibrium point not about sustained periods of economic depression although these too are sometimes misleadingly described as 'cycles'. The proposition is simply that the optimum path back towards equilibrium could typically involve over- and under-shooting rather than a monotonic movement. That is not intuitively unreasonable. Moreover it should be emphasised that the 'optimum' periodicity being discussed is assumed to be predictable and predicted. Trade cycles which are not expected may well be disruptive, but that is a different matter altogether.

The result may be significant also for a 'positive' theory of the trade cycle. Perhaps we observe cycles in the economy because the monetary or fiscal authorities, in their wisdom, have in fact been through a process of reasoning analogous to the one we have described mathematically. Put this way, the idea may seem unrealistic but they could behave 'as if' they had followed this line of reasoning even if it is never made explicit.

The possibility that periodicity in the economy might be induced by the attempt to control it has been a familiar one since at least the 1950s.[5] It does not depend on the authorities making decisions by an explicit process of dynamic optimisation. They may instead follow a simple (although strictly non-optimal) rule of response to the level of activity, its direction of change and the integral of its deviation from some target path. Alternatively, and more plausibly, they may monitor the behaviour of a number of different indicators some of which relate most closely to the level of activity, some to its change and some to its integral. The effect will be much the same, and periodicity could be induced. In fact, rules of this kind may be relatively robust when controlling a system which is changing over time or not fully understood (see Salmon, 1982).

The usefulness of the mathematics derived in this section is not, however, confined to its application to the management of demand by the fiscal or monetary authorities. In the next section we shall see how periodicity could arise in a decentralised or uncontrolled economy.

PERIODICITY WITHOUT CONTROL

In this section the theories discussed will still be very abstract and the question addressed is another very general one. Could periodicity arise in aggregate data as a result of the independent decisions of a multitude of economic agents?

Two rather different models will be considered. First, the analysis of the preceding section can be applied to an individual agent without significant change. The individual's behaviour will then be periodic, but it remains to be seen whether the cycles in individual behaviour could be so synchronised as to produce recognisable periodicity in aggregate. The second model of periodicity depends on the way that agents or groups of agents could interact. We have seen that two first-order difference equations can interact to produce one second-order equation. How is this idea reconciled with optimal decision-making and rational expectations?

The problems of aggregation over a large number of second-order difference equations are quite severe. In other words, one could imagine an economy in which the behaviour of all firms (including their output) was regularly periodic, but the level of aggregate output showed little or no trace of periodicity.

The output of each individual firm can be expressed as

$$y^i = a^i y^i_{-1} + b^i y^i_{-2} + u^i$$

On aggregation one finds a better or worse approximation to a second-order equation

$$y = ay_{-1} + by_{-2} + u$$

where y is an aggregation across y^i, where the parameters a and b are 'some kind of average' of the parameters a^i and b^i and where u is 'some kind of average' of the disturbances u^i. Ease of aggregation depends on the variation across firms in their response parameters and on the extent to which disturbances are common to all. If the firms all belong to a single economy it may be right to expect the disturbance terms u^i to be quite highly correlated across firms. They are all affected by the same disturbances, for example, labour costs, taxation, interest rates, the weather and so on. There seems no reason however to put any restriction on the degree of variation in their response parameters a^i and b^i. These will vary with the size of firm, the techniques of production and stock control used and a whole array of other variables.

Perhaps the best way to illustrate the problems of aggregation in these circumstances is by a simple arithmetical example. In table 3.1 nine successive terms are calculated for a range of eleven second-order difference equations with different frequencies and no damping at all. Thus none of the individual difference equations shows any tendency to settle at the equilibrium at all. They all start off from common initial conditions (corresponding to a disturbance affecting the whole economy). The aver-

Table 3.1. *Aggregation of difference equations, some illustrative calculations*

For each series $y_{-1} = 0$ and $y_0 = 1$

Equations

(a) $y = 0.5y_{-1} - y_{-2}$ (b) $y = 0.6y_{-1} - y_{-2}$ (c) $y = 0.7y_{-1} - y_{-2}$
(d) $y = 0.8y_{-1} - y_{-2}$ (e) $y = 0.9y_{-1} - y_{-2}$ (f) $y = 1.0y_{-1} - y_{-2}$
(g) $y = 1.1y_{-1} - y_{-2}$ (h) $y = 1.2y_{-1} - y_{-2}$ (i) $y = 1.3y_{-1} - y_{-2}$
(j) $y = 1.4y_{-1} - y_{-2}$ (k) $y = 1.5y_{-1} - y_{-2}$

	y_1	y_2	y_3	y_4	y_5	y_6	y_7	y_8	y_9
(a)	0.5	−0.75	−0.88	0.31	1.04	0.21	−0.94	−0.68	0.60
(b)	0.6	−0.64	−0.98	0.05	1.01	0.56	−0.68	−0.97	0.10
(c)	0.7	−0.51	−1.06	−0.23	0.90	0.86	−0.30	−1.07	−0.45
(d)	0.8	−0.36	−1.09	−0.51	0.68	1.06	0.16	−0.93	−0.90
(e)	0.9	−0.19	−1.07	−0.77	0.37	1.11	0.63	−0.55	−1.12
(f)	1.0	−	−1.0	−1.0	−	1.0	1.0	−	−1.0
(g)	1.1	0.21	−0.87	−1.17	−0.41	0.72	1.20	0.60	−0.54
(h)	1.2	0.44	−0.67	−1.24	−0.83	0.25	1.13	1.10	0.20
(i)	1.3	0.69	−0.40	−1.21	−1.18	−0.32	0.76	1.31	0.94
(j)	1.4	0.96	−0.06	−1.04	−1.40	−0.91	0.12	1.08	1.40
(k)	1.5	1.25	0.38	−0.69	−1.41	−1.42	−0.72	0.34	1.23

Average

	y_1	y_2	y_3	y_4	y_5	y_6	y_7	y_8	y_9
	1.0	0.10	−0.70	−0.68	−0.11	0.28	0.21	0.02	0.04

For Comparison: (l) $y = 0.8y_{-1} - 0.65y_{-2}$

| (l) | 0.8 | −0.01 | −0.53 | −0.41 | 0.01 | 0.28 | 0.21 | −0.01 | −0.15 |

age of the eleven series is also calculated. Although the first few terms do suggest some periodicity it is soon blurred, so that one might imagine that quite heavy damping had been applied to the aggregate series. An example is given of a damped second-order system which approximates to the aggregate rather well. If each individual series was itself subject to damping then any impression of periodicity in the aggregate would be easily lost. One must wonder, therefore, how likely it is that observable periodicity could result from the aggregation of periodic behaviour at the level of the individual firm or economic decision taker.

We turn therefore to interaction between two or more decision-takers as a source of periodicity. We revert to the optimisation problem which may face the individual decision taker and suppose that this involves only adjustment costs and not costs associated with cumulated deviations from equilibrium. We have already derived an equation to describe such behaviour.

$$(1 - L)x = -1/\lambda[x^*/(L^{-1} - 1/a)]$$

The adjustment equation for x is first order and adjustment is towards an equilibrium related to the expected future path of x^*.

Now, to see the effects of interaction, suppose that x^* can be replaced by cy where y is a variable controlled by another economic agent. The problem facing that agent may involve costs of adjustment and an equilibrium related to x. Thus the complete interaction system can be described by two equations

$$(1 - aL)x = - cy/(L^{-1} - 1/a)$$

and

$$(1 - bL)y = dx/(L^{-1} - 1/b)$$

These two equations should be solved simultaneously if we believe that the plans of the first agent for x and his expectations for y are consistent with the other agent's expectations for x and his plans for y. These assumptions are strong, but they are required to satisfy the conditions for a 'rational expectations' model.

But these two equations are identical in algebraic form to the equations in x and θ derived in the preceding section to describe the behaviour of a single agent who faces costs related to cumulated output deviations. There is no need therefore to repeat the solution procedure. The same conclusion can be drawn. Both variables x and y will follow paths determined by the same second-order difference equation. The roots of that equation may be complex, but need not be. Therefore periodic behaviour is a possible, but not a necessary, outcome of an interaction of this kind.

The aggregation problems involved in a model of this latter kind are not very severe, especially if we assume that the equilibrium value of each component of x is determined by the average or aggregate of y and *vice versa*. The average derived from a large number of first-order difference equations will itself behave rather like a first-order equation, at least to the extent of moving monotonically towards its equilibrium value. Thus the interaction we have described between two representative agents in deciding the values of x and y will serve also as an explanation of aggregate behaviour.

This seems as far as it is useful to take the argument at this high level of abstraction. The sort of model we now have in mind probably involves the interaction of two or more variables determined independently by different groups of agents. Both decisions involve weighing adjustment costs against costs of being away from some equilibrium. Although lags in the flow of information or the adaptation of expectations could easily be introduced to amplify the model, it is not dependent on such features. It could produce periodicity even in a world of rational expectations, although it is not only in such a world that it will do so. So much for the form of the theory. To make it more concrete the two or more interacting variables must be identified.

In this section we shall assume that the mathematics of periodicity can be described by two interacting first-order difference equations each relating to the behaviour of an aggregate variable. This is a convenient and plausible framework within which to consider a wide range of possible alternatives. The model can be written as

$$y = ay_{-1} + bx_{-1} \qquad \qquad (5a)$$

$$x = cx_{-1} - dy_{-1} \qquad \qquad (5b)$$

The first of the variables responds, with a lag, positively to the second; the second variable responds, with a lag, negatively to the first. Unless one of the 'feedbacks' is positive and the other negative, periodicity cannot arise.

Although periodicity is a phenomenon involving the whole economy it is convenient to begin with the use of these equations to describe the market for a single product. One variable is to represent the quantity produced, output, and the other its price. But which variable is which? And which equation is the demand curve and which the supply curve?

Suppose first that output depends on supply decisions, as for example in an agricultural market, then the first equation will be the supply curve, y is output and x is the price. That leaves the second equation to represent demand conditions with the price falling as supply rises. This model then has affinities to the familiar 'hog-cycle', except that in this model the lag in the adjustment of output to price is a gradual one, rather than a fixed delay, and that prices do not move instantaneously to clear the market.

Since we are more concerned with manufactures than agricultural products in this study and hence with situations of imperfect rather than perfect competition, it is more relevant to consider the case where output is determined by demand. To illustrate this using the same two equations y must be reinterpreted as the price and x as the level of output. The first equation now shows how an increase in output bids up the price which suppliers set (perhaps because their own costs rise) whilst the second equation shows how higher prices cut back demand and hence the level of output.

As the preceding section has shown, a lagged interaction of this kind, producing periodicity in both output and prices, is consistent with rational expectations and optimisation if there are costs involved in making rapid adjustments. For output this should not be a controversial assumption. The idea that there are costs for suppliers in adjusting their prices is more controversial and its basis in theory is less certain. Clearly the two kinds of adjustment do not involve the same kinds of costs (see

Gordon, 1981). (Moreover the experience of hyper-inflation shows that it is not in fact impossible to change prices several times a day if the need is sufficiently pressing.) The stickiness of prices, and also the stickiness of wage costs from which it in part derives, may be due primarily to costs of negotiation. Under imperfect competition where producers set prices, and negotiate wages, there may be advantages in explicit or implicit contracts which inhibit rapid adjustment to new market conditions. This study is not, of course, the place to elaborate this point at any length. It should be noted however that much of what follows is based on the assumption that prices do not always adjust instantaneously.

One can now, quite readily, move from the proposition that equations (5a) and (5b) might represent the market for a manufactured good, to the proposition that they might represent determinants of aggregate output in a market economy. We maintain the position that output variation over the trade cycle corresponds to fluctuations in demand, not supply, which should be reasonably uncontroversial. The first equation is still the supply side, the second still the demand side. The variable x is aggregate output and the variable y represents, in some sense, the price of all output. It is on this last point that we need to pause.

There are several ways in which an increase in prices might feed back to reduce demand. If the money supply (or more generally the stock of financial wealth) is unchanged, then there would be 'real balance' effects on consumption and perhaps also investment demand. Interest rates would rise. If the exchange rate is unchanged then a rise in domestic prices would reduce competitiveness.

If no nominal variables are unchanged, because all assets stocks, all incomes and the exchange rate are effectively indexed, then one must think of y as representing the rate of inflation rather than the price level. Higher inflation, even if it is anticipated, may have depressing effects on the real economy. Higher nominal interest rates, for example, are contractionary in imperfect credit markets. Inflation may lead to productive inefficiency or uncertainty. Inflation redistributes income in a way which may be deflationary. In some respects it is similar to a wealth tax.

One example of the kind of interaction we have just described could be thought of as an application of dynamics to the textbook macroeconomics of the *ISLM* diagram. Equation (5a) represents the *LM* curve with interest rates rising when output is increased. Equation (5b) is the *IS* curve showing how output falls back as a consequence. Just as the application of dynamics to the microeconomic supply and demand curves in a single market can give rise to 'cobwebs' or periodicity, so can a similar treatment of a macroeconomic equilibrium system. Little is required in the way of theoretical innovation. Provided only that some inertia is accepted in the determination of prices as well as quantities, periodicity is easily accommodated within what has been called the 'neo-classical synthesis'.

It is theories of this kind that will form the main basis of the empirical investigation of the trade cycle in Britain in later sections of this study. We shall look for interactions between the level of output on the one hand and the rates of interest and of inflation on the other. Such interactions could, as we have seen, occur in an economy in which no conscious attempts were made by the authorities to 'manage' demand. However, if they do prove important in explaining recent events, this may be because of the way monetary policy (and possibly prices and incomes policy as well) was conducted. One reason, for example, why a rise in inflation depresses demand, may be because policy becomes more contractionary, or because policy is expected to become more contractionary before long.

KEYNESIAN AND MARXIAN MODELS OF THE TRADE CYCLE

No direct mention has been made so far of the trade-cycle models which dominate the literature from the 1930s to the 1960s. Keynes' own discussion of the trade cycle emphasised the role of speculation and the 'animal spirits' of entrepreneurs (see Keynes, 1936, Chapter 22). Later Keynesians elaborated more formal models of periodic cycles which rely on a different kind of mechanism. Many were non-linear but the one which proved most influential was probably the linear multiplier-accelerator model which became the basis for much of the postwar discussion of 'counter-cyclical' policy.

The essential feature of these models is the accelerator rather than the multiplier. All the variations on the theme involve interaction between the level of output and a variable with the dimensions of a stock, either the 'stock of stocks' or the stock of fixed capital. No important role is given to prices, or inflation, or the rate of interest. Output is determined by demand and the demand for output includes the demand for additions to the capital stock. This mechanism is potentially a source of periodic fluctuations.

Initially one needs four equations

$$y = ay_{-1} + i \tag{6a}$$

$$i = \lambda(K^*_{-1} - K_{-1}) \tag{6b}$$

$$K = vK_{-1} + i \tag{6c}$$

$$K^* = by \tag{6d}$$

The first equation relates output, y, to consumer demand (which is proportional to last period's output) and investment. Investment, in the second equation, represents adjustment towards a desired capital stock. The third equation shows how investment augments the stock. The fourth equation, which is crucial, says that the desired stock of capital depends on output.

With some simplification, this system can be reduced to two equations, in output and the capital stock, of the same form as equations (5a) and (5b). The capital stock adjusts positively, with a lag, to the level of output; the level of output in turn adjusts negatively, with a lag, to the size of the existing stock of capital. The result could be a periodic cycle.

It is important to note that the variables involved are aggregates. The output of each individual firm depends not just, or even mainly, on the stock of fixed or working capital held by the firm itself. Indeed firms do not typically produce their own fixed capital at all. There is a market in this model which integrates the activities of the economy even though no price variable has a role to play. For this reason the aggregation problems mentioned in an earlier section of this study do not arise. (This is true even if the second equation relating capital requirements to the level of output does work at the level of the individual firm rather than the industry or the economy as a whole.)

The earlier discussion of optimisation does suggest one issue of which the multiplier-accelerator models may not have taken sufficient account. In equation (6d) capital requirements are related to output in the current period. Given that there are costs of adjusting capital and also some flexibility in production, there may be little incentive to vary the capital stock significantly over the phases of a cycle which is known to be periodic. We have already remarked that there is not much sign of fixed capital variation over the seasons of the year (although stock levels do vary). It is theoretically possible for an accelerator cycle to be induced although expectations are fully rational. However, the use of the model described here has in practice often been associated with the assumption, tacit or open, that expectations are rather crudely adaptive, with the current level of output treated as if it were the best estimate of the long-run equilibrium.

Since the 1960s a number of substantial macroeconomic models have been constructed of the American, British and other economies, all broadly using the Keynesian tradition, at least as a starting point. These models typically incorporate both a 'multiplier' and an 'accelerator', and in consequence show some trace of periodicity caused by the mechanism described in this section. The study of periodicity in large macroeconomic models is discussed briefly in the next section.

Marxian models of the trade cycle are less familiar than Keynesian ones, but they are currently the subject of revived, rather specialist, interest (see Goodwin, Krüger and Vercelli, 1984). The term will be used here to describe a rather general class of models, not all of which would perhaps be properly described as Marxian. The identifying characteristic is the importance attached to the distribution of income. In fact, the mechanisms involved will be found in many models more usually called Keynesian or even neo-classical.

There is no need to dwell here on the issue of linearity or non-linearity, which has been touched on already. Many proponents of what I have called Marxian models would attach considerable importance to non-linearity and adopt a mathematical form for their theory which would produce a limit cycle. But this is a possibility for all the theories we have discussed, not a feature which distinguishes what are here called Marxian theories from the rest.

A Marxian model of periodicity can be represented as the interaction of two equations of a now familiar kind

$$y = ay_{-1} - bw_{-1}$$
$$w = cw_{-1} + dy_{-1}$$

in this case y is the level of output and w is the share of labour in total income. The first equation relates the growth of output, negatively, to the labour share. This is because growth depends on investment and investment depends on the rate of profit. The second equation relates the growth of the labour share to the level of output either directly or through the effect of output on the level of unemployment. It may be given a Marxian interpretation, but as an empirical observation it is little different from the wage equations (or 'augmented Phillips' curves') found, with more or less theoretical justification, in most large macroeconomic models.

The main reservation about using such a model to explain a cycle of around five years' duration in the British economy is the time-scale involved in the mechanism of the first equation. Surely the effect of investment on the productive capacity of the economy is too slow to explain fluctuations with that frequency. Moreover the trade cycle which we observe in the British economy since the war is a cycle in demand relative to capacity (see chart 1.1). It is only to a much more limited extent, if at all, a cycle in productive potential or in capacity.

This does not mean, however, that the distribution of income cannot be invoked as part of a trade-cycle mechanism. The first equation can be reinterpreted as an equation for the demand for output, not the supply side. It is sometimes suggested that a redistribution of income from profits to wages will increase demand, but this could be reversed in an open economy. The variable, w, could, in effect, stand for both the labour share and international competitiveness. Such a model could, if the parameters had the right values, be used to explain a cycle of around five years' duration in demand. Whether it is, in fact, viable as an explanation of recent experience in this country depends of course on what has actually happened to competitiveness over that period, which will be discussed in a later part of this study.

STUDYING CYCLES IN LARGE MACROECONOMIC MODELS

Before concluding the theoretical part of this study a brief note may be appropriate on the usefulness of large macroeconomic models to investigate the trade cycle and its possible periodicity. This is perhaps especially appropriate as the author is a firm believer in the usefulness of large, or fairly large, macroeconomic models for such purposes as forecasting and policy analysis, yet little use will be made of them in this study.

There is a quite substantial specialist literature, mainly dating from the 1960s, about the cyclical properties of large macroeconomic models, mainly models of the American economy.[6] As these are large, complicated non-linear systems, it may require a lot of painstaking work to answer apparently quite easy questions about their properties.

With some rather hazardous linearisation and approximation the determination of any individual variable within a large macroeconomic model can be written as

$$y = a^1 y_{-1} + a^2 y_{-2} + \ldots + b^{10} z^1 + b^{11} z^1_{-1} + \ldots$$
$$+ b^{20} z^2 + b^{21} z^2_{-1} + \ldots + c^{10} u^1 + c^{11} u^1_{-1} + \ldots$$
$$+ c^{20} u^2 + c^{21} u^2_{-1} + \ldots$$

That is to say, the variable depends on its own lagged values and the current or lagged values of all the exogenous variables and disturbances in the whole model. Earlier sections of this study have described how periodicity can arise in a linear stochastic difference equation. It can be implicit in the pattern of coefficients on the lagged values of the dependent variable (the a coefficients); alternatively, the independent variables, including those unobservable variables which contribute to the error term, may themselves be periodic. Something akin to periodicity could also occur as a result of a 'cyclical' pattern in the b or c coefficients. It is perhaps only correct to speak of periodicity as being explained by the model if it is inherent in the a coefficients since it is these that summarise the interactions between endogenous variables which the model has been able to identify. One approach to the investigation of periodicity within large models is therefore the calculation of these coefficients and the solution of the corresponding polynomial equation in the lag operator. Periodicity would be indicated by the finding of complex roots of the right frequency with little damping. (These roots will be common to the polynomial equations defined by the a coefficients of all endogenous variables in the model.)

An alternative method of analysing the properties of large models is by 'simulation'. As a matter of routine, anyone seeking to understand a model, including its builders, will trace out the consequences for the most interesting endogenous variables, such as output or employment, of making changes in the more interesting exogenous variables, such as public spending or the level of world trade. If the a coefficients of the model imply periodicity this will be immediately evident from the results of such simulations.

As we have seen, the path traced by an endogenous variable in response to any single disturbance is, in a linear system, also the path traced out by the autocorrelation coefficients when the system is subjected to a 'white noise' disturbance. These coefficients show the strength of periodicity in a stochastic environment. A change to an exogenous variable is in effect one such disturbance (except that the signal may be confused if the b coefficients imply a multiple rather than a single disturbance when the exogenous variable changes).

Table 3.2 shows the results of two simulations using the National Institute model of the British economy. In neither of them is there any marked evidence of periodicity in the response of output. There is some trace of an inventory cycle, with a period of about five years, but it is so modest in its effects on total output as to be barely perceptible. The behaviour of fixed investment differs markedly as between the two simulations quoted. These results are not unrepresentative. Most simulations of this kind suggest that the British, and the American, economy is not inherently periodic.[7]

One might be tempted to bring this whole study to an abrupt close at that point, but that would be too hasty a response. It is possible (if unlikely) that modelbuilders have missed some key relationship in the British economy which could be uncovered by an investigation centred on the explanation of periodicity. Perhaps the behaviour of stocks and fixed investment has a much more pronounced effect on the path of output. More persuasively, it could be argued that models which take fiscal and monetary policy, including interest rates, as exogenous, may for that reason fail to uncover a mechanism which generates quite regular cycles. Moreover, the investigation would be worth continuing if only to find out why it is that the course of output since 1959 seems to be regularly periodic, even if it is not.

The simulations referred to so far are 'deterministic' or 'non-stochastic'

Table 3.2. *Simulations of the National Institute model*

£m at 1980 prices

	(1)			(2)		
	Gross Domestic Product	Stock-building	Fixed Investment	Gross Domestic Product	Stock-building	Fixed Investment
Q1	360	20	12	285	71	16
2	429	65	15	303	114	32
3	444	95	30	304	118	48
4	430	80	22	280	91	59
5	458	54	10	254	56	67
6	460	43	2	229	24	71
7	471	35	−5	209	−2	68
8	486	30	−3	198	−17	61
9	491	27	−8	196	−21	56
10	492	22	−13	200	−18	54
11	498	17	−5	202	−13	54
12	496	14	−3	203	−9	54
13	497	11	−3	207	−7	54
14	504	9	−2	197	−6	52
15	512	9	1	191	−7	49
16	520	12	6	186	−9	46
17	529	16	13	182	−10	42
18	542	18	21	179	−11	38
19	554	20	31	176	−10	35
20	561	22	43	175	−10	31
21	563	20	54	175	−8	27
22	566	16	63	176	−6	25
23	568	12	71	176	−5	22
24	567	9	80	177	−3	19

Source: NIESR Model 7. A full account of these and other simulations is given in Henry and Johns (1985).

(1) Public consumption raised by £400m a quarter at 1980 prices.
(2) The volume of world trade raised by 5 per cent.

but they have been used as the basis for deduction about the behaviour of the models in response to stochastic perturbations. It is possible to explore such behaviour of the models more directly by 'stochastic' simulations. This involves repeated calculations of the effect on endogenous variables of randomly selected 'shocks' to the error terms in the model equations or the exogenous variables, or both.

As one would expect, the results of such simulations do not, as a rule, provide clear evidence of periodicity. The fact that something like periodicity is sometimes observed is probably to be explained by the interaction of the a coefficients, which on their own are not periodic, with the b and c coefficients (or the autoregressive structure of the error terms generated for the simulations themselves if these are not 'white noise'). The results of such interaction cannot be a simple periodicity of the kind shown by a univariate linear difference equation dominated by a pair of complex roots. Nevertheless, there could be combinations of autoregressive and moving-average terms which produce output that looks quite regularly periodic especially in small samples.

That said, most of the studies based on stochastic simulations have not been concerned with periodicity directly, but with the average duration of trade cycles. In the early studies this was based on counting the average time between turning points in the data generated by the simulation exercise.[8] It is of some interest to compare this average duration with the average duration of a trade cycle in the real world. But it is not strictly relevant to the question of periodicity with which we are concerned here.

THE CYCLE AND THE TREND

We have discussed the trade cycle up to this point as if there were no ambiguity about what it means. That indeed is the impression one gets from looking at the chart shown in the introduction. But the series drawn on that chart were in fact selected because they are relatively free of an ambiguity which affects most others.

The problems of distinguishing trend from cycle are not the same for all variables. In an interrelated system the cycle is the same for all, but the trends of different variables may be quite different, and arise for quite different reasons. We shall take three examples: the price level, the level of output and the level of unemployment. The price level, notoriously, has been rising continuously since the early 1950s. It is obviously not a stationary series in the sense that statisticians use the term. But it is not obvious whether it is stationary about an exogenous rising trend or stationary as a rate of change. If there exists, as some economists would maintain, an exogenous nominal magnitude in the real world (for example, the money supply or the exchange rate or even wages) and that determines the equilibrium price level, then the first characterisation is correct: the price level is stationary about a rising trend. If, however, the money supply, the exchange rate and wages are all, in the long run, endogenous, then the absolute level of prices may be indeterminate. In that case the second characterisation may be correct, with the rate of inflation stationary, but the price level non-stationary. The two represent quite different theories of the determination of prices, but they may be quite difficult to distinguish in practice.[9] In the present context this means we might be interested either in the cyclical behaviour of prices around a rising trend or the cyclical behaviour of the rate of inflation. If one is periodic, so is the other; but if the trend rise is inappropriately treated in estimation, the frequency and damping of the cycle will be obscured.

The idea that the level of prices is indeterminate in the long run is familiar, if not altogether uncontroversial. The idea that the level of output is indeterminate is more of a challenge. It may, nevertheless, have its supporters. If returns to extra investment are not decreasing, one could envisage a case in which the demand for output adjusted towards supply, but at the same time the supply of output adjusted towards the demand. If Δ is a difference operator

$$F(\Delta)s = \lambda(s - d)$$

$$G(\Delta)d = \mu(d - s)$$

The solution of these two equations is a difference equation in the growth rate of output, the level being indeterminate. As for prices, if this indeterminacy is accepted, the cycle to be investigated is a cycle in the growth rate of output not in its level relative to its trend.

Until quite recently it would have been axiomatic that unemployment was a stationary series, reflecting (even defining) the cycle and free of any trend. Since the late 1960s this is no longer certain. There has been an almost uninterrupted upward movement in unemployment for two decades. In this study that increase is not regarded as a trade cycle at all, although this does not mean that the cause of the trend rise in unemployment is not demand deficiency.

There are two possibilities. The first is that some exogenous variable (say the decline of the 'work ethic' whatever that means) accounts for the trend rise and unemployment is therefore stationary about a rising trend. The alternative is that the 'equilibrium' or 'natural' rate of unemployment is itself influenced by the history of actual unemployment (because for example experience of unemployment undermines the 'work ethic'). If so, the same dynamic structure applies as has been applied to the cases of prices and output. The long-run level of unemployment is indeterminate and the cycle is in the change in unemployment not its level.

It may be said that the trend movements in prices, and in output and unemployment, are much more deserving of study than the trade cycle. That may be true. Nevertheless, so far as this study is concerned, trends are important only because they interfere with the correct perception of periodicity. In Chapters 4 and 5 of this study careful attention will have to be given to this problem.

CONCLUSIONS

The ground has now been laid for an examination of the data. The main point to come out of this preliminary discussion of theory is that periodicity as such would not be a very surprising or even a very significant phenomenon to observe. There are lots and lots of theoretical models within which it is a possibility and few which would confidently exclude it.

It is not appropriate therefore to treat periodicity as if it were itself a hypothesis which should be tested. In a very simple model, a second-order difference equation for example, one can speak of periodicity as being either present or absent depending on whether the roots of the characteristic equation are complex or real. But such a simple model is of course no more than an approximation. When speaking of the real world we can only treat periodicity as a matter of degree. We could estimate a second-order equation with no complex roots, even if the real world in fact was a system with many complex roots provided they were all so heavily damped as to have little influence on the general pattern of the trade cycle. We shall not in this study therefore be asking whether the cycle is periodic or not, but rather trying to estimate how periodic it is. This turns out to be quite a difficult task in its own right.

It has been, one hopes, interesting and illuminating to review some of the interactions of economic behaviour which might contribute to periodicity. The result, however, is a multiplicity of alternatives; and the account has been by no means exhaustive. Nevertheless, a study which seeks to explain periodicity must try to discriminate. Particular attention will be devoted to the kind of model which has been described as consistent with the 'neo-classical synthesis'. Here aggregate output interacts with prices, or with the rates of interest and of inflation. The role of economic policy and world output will also be investigated. As we have seen the dynamic structure of such a model depends in part on the way expectations are formed, but periodicity is consistent with either adaptive or rational expectations. We shall not on this occasion attempt to model expectations directly. But this is to anticipate Chapters 5 and 6. Our immediate concern is with the measurement of periodicity and the assessment of its importance to the character of the trade cycle. That is the subject of Chapter 4.

4

OBSERVATION AND MEASUREMENT OF
PERIODICITY

Trade-cycle theory does not lead to a confident prediction either that periodicity will, or will not, occur. If periodicity has been little studied recently it is not because it can be dismissed on *a priori* grounds. The neglect of the phenomenon seems rather to be due to the belief that it seldom, if ever, actually occurs. A recent American textbook, for example, seems quite confident that cycles are not periodic.[1] A recent American journal article on business cycle theory, which is exceptional in that it mentions periodicity at all, does so only to dismiss it as empirically unimportant.[2] It is uncomfortable to find oneself confronted by widespread scepticism about the very existence of the phenomenon under study. Nevertheless, one should approach the evidence with an open mind. The first section of this chapter will consider some questions of definition and methodology. What exactly is meant by periodicity? How would one recognise it? The second section will review the evidence of periodicity in annual data for Britain before the first world war and for America and Britain since 1960. The third section will examine periodicity in Britain since 1960 in much more detail, using quarterly data.

METHODOLOGY

The student of the trade cycle usually begins by looking at turning points, peaks and troughs, followed perhaps by an examination of 'upcrosses' and 'downcrosses', the points at which the series crosses its mean value or its trendline. The time elapsed between corresponding points of successive cycles is the measure of cycle length. Periodicity can then be defined as a tendency for the distribution of cycle lengths to peak at a particular value. This, it seems, is what the 'plain man' would mean if he said that cycles tend to be about (say) five years in duration. He would mean that the *typical* cycle was about that long, not merely that it was the average length of all cycles.

One difficulty should be apparent immediately. If one has, say, twenty-five years of data, about the time-span often used in the estimation of econometric models, and if the typical duration of a cycle is in fact about five years, then one will observe only about four or five peaks and troughs.

That does not provide much of a basis for constructing a frequency distribution. If, on the other hand, one uses data for a much longer period then it is unlikely that the underlying structure of the economy which determines whether periodicity occurs, and what the typical cycle length is, will remain unchanged within the sample period. This is especially true when the economy has been disturbed by major wars and their aftermath, as it was for the first half of the present century. The problem of statistical degrees of freedom is not as severe in studying the trade cycle as it is for those who explore 'long waves', but it is very severe nevertheless.

Analysis of turning points or up- and downcrosses uses only a small proportion of the information contained in a data series. The calculation of autocorrelation coefficients makes use of all the observations and takes account of the degree of regularity at all phases in the cycle. When data series are short, however, the problems of interpretation remain. It is certainly hazardous to calculate correlations between observations ten years apart when one has only, say, twenty-five years of data. In a smooth and regular cycle (of any shape or asymmetry) one would find a high degree of positive correlation between observations separated by one or more cycle lengths. In between there would probably be negative correlations (but this would depend on the shape as well as the regularity of the cycle). In practice, autocorrelations from even quite large samples tend to be uneven and difficult to interpret.

The transformation of the autocorrelation function into the spectral density enables one to combine in an appropriate way estimates of autocorrelations over a range much longer than the length of a typical cycle. It is rightly a standard practice to calculate the spectrum of a series when investigating periodicity in large samples. In small samples its interpretation is often problematic (see Harvey, 1981, Chapter 3). If one has few observations on which to base estimates of autocorrelations over periods which are long relative to the length of a typical cycle, then spectral analysis is unlikely to reveal much which is not discoverable from inspection of the low-order terms in the autocorrelation function or indeed from inspection of the data series itself.

The calculation of autoregressions can be seen as just another way of describing the behaviour of a data series. Any series with regular periodicity will tend to produce estimates of autoregression parameters appropriate to a linear difference equation with complex roots implying periodicity with about the correct cycle length. This is true even of data generated by a very non-linear model (an example is given in Blatt, 1978). One could use autoregressions as an indirect means of estimating autocorrelation functions or spectral shape. In this way the cyclical properties of the estimated linear difference equation could be used as estimates of the cyclical properties suggested by the data.

It is a small, but crucial, step from this to the view that a relatively low-order linear stochastic difference equation is in fact the best representation of the data generating process. A previous section of this study has suggested that this is, in the context of some theoretical models of the trade cycle, a natural and appropriate step to take.

A standard regression model does not distinguish between errors of observation and 'disturbances' which represent omitted variables. In some contexts this does not matter, but in estimating time-series models it may matter a great deal. The linear stochastic model of the trade cycle implies that the amplitude and phase of the cycle, as opposed to its frequency and damping, depend on the character of the disturbances to which it is subjected. This is one reason why an explicit error model, probably including a moving-average component, is likely to be important to the identification of the time-series models which best represent the trade cycle.

More sophisticated error models may be appropriate for other reasons. The theory, sketched out in the previous section of this study, does not in general point to second differences as direct influences on behaviour. The true underlying behavioural equations are perhaps better specified as the result of interaction between two or more related variables. If so, as was mentioned in Chapter 2 above, the derived equations involving second differences will not have white noise error terms. Some of the results reported below, using quarterly data for the United Kingdom, make use of a moving average estimation programme.

Any method of studying periodicity involves distinguishing the trade cycle being studied from the trend around which it takes place. A simple count of turning points or 'up-' and 'downcrosses' turns out to be one of the more robust techniques in this respect, provided that the amplitude of the cycle is large relative to the gradient of the trend. For twenty years after the second world war, however, the output trend was so rapid in many countries, and the cycle so attenuated, that cycles in growth rates of output were the subject of study rather than cycles in its level. The appropriate level of differencing, however, depends on theory, or on the properties of the observed estimation errors, not on convenience. The theoretical arguments have been rehearsed in Chapter 3 of this study. An inappropriate choice of time trends may distort out of all recognition the shape of the cycle. This is true not only of regression estimates but also of methods using autocorrelation or spectral analysis. For example, it is a familiar observation that growth rates in most, perhaps all, western countries slowed down in the 1970s compared with the 1960s. An attempt to fit a stable time-series model across both decades without including any variable to explain this feature of the data would almost inevitably distort the shorter-term dynamics of output behaviour.

The danger that a random walk for example will be misinterpreted as fluctuation around an exogenous trend is well documented (see Nelson and Plosser, 1982). The argument seems perfectly symmetrical with just as real a danger that fluctuations about an exogenous trend will be misinterpreted as a random walk. The appropriate decomposition of economic time series into trend and cyclical components has been the subject of an interesting debate in the last few years. It is possible to estimate a general model from which deterministic or stochastic trends can emerge as special cases. Within this framework two alternatives can be considered: that there is a cycle around an independent trend or that the growth rate of the series is itself cyclical. An appropriate method of estimation, based on the Kalman filter, has been developed by Professor Harvey (1985), and an example of its use is reported below.

UNEMPLOYMENT IN BRITAIN 1851–1913

Table 4.1 shows the percentage unemployed in all trade unions for which information is available, annually from 1851 to 1913. (In the later decades more trade unions kept records so the series is not consistent in coverage over the whole period.)

The peaks and troughs listed in the table suggest that the cyclical behaviour of the British economy may not have been entirely uniform for the whole 60-year period. In the 1850s there were several short cycles followed by a long period of rather longer cycles in the range seven to eleven years which continued until the turn of the century. The period from 1869 to 1900 in Britain is indeed the *locus classicus* of trade-cycle theory, although the interpretation of even this piece of history as an example of systematic periodicity is open to question.[3] The autocovariances up to a ten-year lag are shown in the table. These suggest quite a regular periodic pattern. There are negative covariances around three to five years which is half a cycle, and positive covariances around six to ten years which is a whole cycle. The estimates of the spectrum, which are also tabulated, seem on this occasion to discriminate rather more finely. There are in fact two spectral peaks, one at about $5\frac{1}{2}$ years, the other at about $8\frac{1}{2}$ years, with quite a deep trough in between. This is consistent with the distribution of turning points that has already been described.

The autoregression in levels gives quite clear evidence of periodicity (with a 't' statistic of 3.7 attached to the coefficient on unemployment lagged two years). The irregular character of the cycle for part of the period is interpreted as evidence of a rather 'damped' cycle. The cycle length is estimated at $6\frac{1}{2}$ years. This is considerably lower than the rough

Table 4.1. *Unemployment in the United Kingdom, 1851–1913*

Data: Trade Union members unemployed (per cent)						
	1860 1.9	1870 3.9	1880 5.5	1890 2.1	1900 2.5	1910 4.7
1851 3.9	1 5.2	1 1.6	1 2.1	1 3.5	1 3.3	11 3.0
2 6.0	2 8.4	2 0.9	2 2.3	2 6.3	2 4.0	12 3.2
3 1.7	3 6.0	3 1.2	3 2.6	3 7.5	3 4.7	13 2.1
4 2.9	4 2.7	4 1.7	4 8.1	4 6.9	4 6.0	
5 5.4	5 2.1	5 2.4	5 9.3	5 5.8	5 5.0	
6 4.7	6 3.3	6 3.7	6 10.2	6 3.3	6 3.6	
7 6.0	7 7.4	7 4.7	7 7.6	7 3.3	7 3.7	
8 11.9	8 7.9	8 6.8	8 4.6	8 2.8	8 7.8	
9 3.8	9 6.7	9 11.4	9 2.1	9 2.0	9 7.7	

Source: The Abstract of British Historical Statistics.

Peaks	Years between	Peaks	Years between	Troughs	Years between	Troughs	Years between
1852		1886	7	1853		1882	10
1855	3	1893	7	1856	3	1889/90	7/8
1858	3	1904	11	1860	4	1899	9/10
1862	4	1908	4	1865	5	1906	7
1868	6	1912	4	1872	7	1911	5
1879	11						

Covariances (years of lag)

0	1	2	3	4	5	6	7	8	9	10
6.2	3.2	−0.3	−1.9	−2.0	−1.0	0.3	0.7	0.5	0.4	0.2

Spectrum (period in years)

3	$3\frac{1}{2}$	4	$4\frac{1}{2}$	5	$5\frac{1}{2}$	6	$6\frac{1}{2}$	7	$7\frac{1}{2}$	8	$8\frac{1}{2}$	9	$9\frac{1}{2}$	10
0.5	0.6	0.6	0.6	1.5	3.5	2.1	1.1	3.0	4.4	5.1	5.2	4.1	3.0	2.0

Regressions (standard errors in parentheses)

1853–1913

(1) $y = 3.65 + 0.75y_{-1} - 0.43y_{-2} + 0.01t$
     (0.80) (9.12)   (0.12)   (0.01)

$SE = 2.00$ $\bar{R}^2 = 0.40$ $DW = 2.0$ *Cycle length*: 6.5 years

(2) $\Delta y = 0.07 + 0.11\Delta y_{-1} - 0.31\Delta y_{-2}$
      (0.31) (0.12)   (0.12)

$SE = 2.39$ $\bar{R}^2 = 0.08$ $DW = 2.0$ *Cycle length*: 4.3 years

1862–1913

(1) $y = 2.58 + 0.96y_{-1} - 0.54y_{-2} + 0.002t$
     (0.81) (0.12)   (0.12)   (0.016)

$SE = 1.65$ $\bar{R}^2 = 0.56$ $DW = 2.1$ *Cycle length*: 7.3 years

(2) $\Delta y = -0.10 + 0.34\Delta y_{-1} - 0.30\Delta y_{-2}$
      (0.28)   (0.14)   (0.13)

$SE = 2.01$ $\bar{R}^2 = 0.12$ $DW = 2.1$ *Cycle length*: 5.0 years

figure of ten years often used to describe the classical British trade cycle, but compares well with an average interval of six years between peaks shown in the earlier part of the table. The results for a regression which starts at 1862 are also reported. The fit is rather better over this shorter period and the cycle length is, as one might expect, a little longer.

The regressions in differences do not seem to tell quite the same story. They fit very badly with a higher standard error. They suggest an even more damped cycle and also an even shorter one with a cycle length of only $4\frac{1}{2}$ or 5 years.

The estimation models described in Harvey (1985) were applied to the same data series. The results were broadly consistent with those already described using less sophisticated techniques (although their interpretation is a little clouded by a rather high level of heteroscedasticity). The main results were as follows:

	ρ	λ	w
Case (1): Trend plus cycle	0.74	0.80	7.9
Case (2): Cyclical trend	0.87	0.99	6.3

The first parameter (ρ) determines the stability or regularity of the cycles with a value close to unity indicating a cycle close to the boundary of the 'explosive' region. The second parameter (λ) determines the frequency of the cycle. From this the cycle length in years (w) can be calculated directly. The estimates, about eight years for the 'trend plus cycle' model and about $6\frac{1}{2}$ years for the 'cyclical trend' model are a little longer than those estimated by the simple autoregressions reported above. It is encouraging, however, to find that the conclusions based on simple autoregressions are not, in this case at least, much modified when a more comprehensive model is estimated.

UNEMPLOYMENT IN THE UNITED KINGDOM AND THE UNITED STATES SINCE 1960

The 1960s and the 1970s provide a run of reasonably homogenous data undisturbed by major wars in the main western industrial countries. Trade-cycle fluctuations recurred despite 'counter-cyclical' policies, but their amplitude was much reduced compared with those of the nineteenth century, and economic activity very stable if compared with the prolonged depression of the interwar years. Quarterly data for the United Kingdom are analysed in greater detail elsewhere in this paper. In this section the main concern is to put the British experience of this period in its historical and geographical setting, contrasting it with the 'classical' cycle of the late nineteenth century and also with the contemporary experience of America. The evidence is set out in tables 4.2 and 4.3.

Despite a strong upward trend in the 1970s the peaks and troughs of the level of unemployment in the United Kingdom give quite a clear impression of the cycle. There were four cycles between 1961 and 1979,

Table 4.2. *Unemployment in the United Kingdom 1960–81*

(Per cent) (on internationally standardised basis)				
1960 2.1	1965 2.1	1970 3.1	1975 4.6	1980 7.4
1 1.9	6 2.2	1 3.9	6 6.0	1 11.0
2 2.7	7 3.2	2 4.2	7 6.3	
3 3.3	8 3.2	3 3.2	8 6.3	
4 2.4	9 3.0	4 3.1	9 5.7	

Source: Report of the US President, 1982.

Peaks	Years between	Troughs	Years between
1963		1961	
1967/8	4/5	1965	4
1977/8	5/6	1969	4
		1974	5
		1979	5

Covariances

(years of lag)	0	1	2	3	4	5	6	7
(in levels)	0.8	0.4	0.1	0.1	0.2	0.2	−0.1	−0.3
(in differences)	0.9	0.4	−0.4	−0.3	0.1	0.3	0.1	−0.2

Spectral Peaks (in levels) 20 years and 4.4 years
(in differences) 4.7 years

Regressions (standard errors in parentheses)
(1a) $y = -0.33 + 1.23y_{-1} - 0.65y_{-2} + 0.17t$
    (0.63) (0.33)   (0.36)   (0.09)

$SE = 0.95$ $\bar{R}^2 = 0.82$ $DW = 1.2$ *Cycle length*: 8.9 years

(1b) $y = 5.56 + 0.56y_{-1} - 1.03y_{-2} - 0.52t + 0.04t^2$
    (1.26) (0.25)   (0.24)   (0.15)   (0.01)

$SE = 0.59$ $\bar{R}^2 = 0.93$ $DW = 1.5$ *Cycle length*: 4.9 years

(2a) $\Delta y = 0.45 + 0.56\Delta y_{-1} - 0.91\Delta y_{-2}$
    (0.21) (0.25)   (0.28)

$SE = 0.83$ $\bar{R}^2 = 0.41$ $DW = 1.6$ *Cycle length*: 4.8 years

(2b) $\Delta y = -0.62 + 0.44\Delta y_{-1} - 0.96\Delta y_{-2} + 0.09t$
    (0.40) (0.21)   (0.23)   (0.03)

$SE = 0.68$ $\bar{R}^2 = 0.60$ $DW = 2.4$ *Cycle length*: 4.7 years

two of about four years followed by two of about five years. Only three cycles can be distinguished for the United States in this way, one of four years, one of six and one of seven.

The covariances and spectral peaks have been calculated both for levels and for differences or changes in the rate of unemployment. The latter series show a much clearer pattern, because in both countries, but especially in the United Kingdom, the trend of unemployment is

Table 4.3. *Unemployment in the United States 1960–81*

Data (Per cent) (on internationally standardised basis)				
1960 5.5	1965 4.5	1970 4.9	1975 8.5	1980 7.1
1 6.7	6 3.8	1 5.9	6 7.7	1 7.6
2 5.5	7 3.8	2 5.6	7 7.1	
3 5.7	8 3.6	3 4.9	8 6.1	
4 5.2	9 3.5	4 5.6	9 5.8	

Source: Report of the US President, 1982.

Peaks	Years between	Troughs	Years between
1961		1962	
1963	2	1969	7
1971	8	1973	4
1975	4	1979	6

Covariances

(Years of lag)	0	1	2	3	4	5	6	7
(in levels)	1.3	0.8	0.3	–	–	−0.1	−0.4	−0.6
(in differences)	0.9	0.1	−0.3	−0.2	−0.1	0.2	−0.1	−0.1

Spectral Peaks (In levels) 14 years and 4.9 years
(In differences) 5.0 years

Regressions (Standard errors in parentheses)
(1a) $y = 1.63 + 0.76y_{-1} - 0.26y_{-2} + 0.09t$
  (0.92) (0.25) (0.22) (0.05)

$SE = 0.89$ $\bar{R}^2 = 0.64$ $DW = 1.8$ *Cycle length*: 8.6 years

(1b) $y = 2.89 + 0.76y_{-1} - 0.34y_{-2} - 0.07t + 0.07t^2$
  (1.93) (0.25) (0.24) (0.23) (0.09)

$SE = 0.90$ $\bar{R}^2 = 0.63$ $DW = 1.8$ *Cycle length*: 6.7 years

(2a) $\Delta y = 0.11 + 0.14\Delta y_{-1} - 0.29\Delta y_{-2}$
  (0.23) (0.23) (0.23)

$SE = 0.99$ $\bar{R}^2 = -0.03$ $DW = 2.0$ *Cycle length*: 4.4 years

(2b) $\Delta y = -0.27 + 0.10\Delta y_{-1} - 0.29\Delta y_{-2} + 0.03t$
  (0.61) (0.24) (0.23) (0.04)

$SE = 1.00$ $\bar{R}^2 = -0.04$ $DW = 2.0$ *Cycle length*: 4.2 years

different in the 1970s from the 1960s. The calculations in levels interpret this as part of a very long cycle, about twenty years in the case of the United Kingdom, fourteen years in the case of the United States. Obviously there is not enough data here to form a judgement about the existence of cycles of that length, so the optimistic view implied about the nature of the upward trend in unemployment in both countries should not be given any weight at all.

Of more significance is the indication of trade-cycle periodicity in both countries with a frequency around $4\frac{1}{2}$ to 5 years. In the case of the United Kingdom data the covariances in differences correspond quite closely to those generated by a second-order difference equation and the spectrum correspondingly has a single clearly-defined peak. But for the shortage of observations, and hence of degrees of freedom, this would be a very impressive demonstration of periodicity.

The results for the United States data also show some evidence of periodicity. The covariances in differences follow a pattern similar to that in the United Kingdom data although they fall away towards zero rather more rapidly as the lag length is extended. The spectral peak is again quite clearly defined, although in this case there is a suggestion of a subsidiary peak around $2\frac{1}{2}$ years. These results again are consistent with the observation we have made of turning points. Given the short run of data it might indeed be questioned whether they add much to the impression which can be made with the 'naked eye'.

The regression estimates for the United Kingdom data confirm its periodicity. To get a clear picture it is necessary to take account of the acceleration in unemployment by adding a term in 'time squared'; in fact the upward trend is usually understood to have got under way around the end of the 1960s. If only a simple trend is included the cycle is estimated (implausibly) as having a period of nearly nine years. If unemployment is differenced, or if a quadratic trend is included, the coefficient on unemployment lagged two periods is close to unity, in one case actually over unity. This indicates a periodic cycle which is very regular and on the very borderline of instability. The period is estimated at nearly five years, which corresponds well with the observed peaks and troughs. The standard error is lowest in the levels equation that includes a quadratic time trend. The fit of both the equations in changes is nevertheless quite good.

The regression estimates for the United States also suggest an element of periodicity, but the evidence is relatively weak and doubtful. One can perhaps understand why American economists lost interest in periodicity or even became quite confident of its non-occurrence during the 1960s and 1970s. With or without a quadratic time trend, whether in levels or changes, one could not reject the hypothesis that American unemployment follows a first order dynamic process. Even if, nevertheless, the estimates of cycle lengths are taken at face value, they do not provide a well-defined picture. The cycle may be $8\frac{1}{2}$ years, or nearly 7, or perhaps about 4 or $4\frac{1}{2}$ years, depending on which version of the regression equation one prefers. The equations in changes fit so badly that the R^2 adjusted for degrees of freedom is actually negative. In fact both the equations in changes would quite naturally be interpreted as random walks.

A very influential article, Granger (1966), reported that most data series for the United States, when analysed over periods extending back to the beginning of the century, did not yield spectral peaks in the 'business cycle frequencies'. More recently results of a similar kind are quoted in Sargent (1979) using quarterly data from 1949 to 1976. The spectral analysis reported here does not conflict with these results, but may warn against their generalisation to all countries and all time periods. The results summarised by Granger span two world wars and the crash of 1929, events which undoubtedly upset any tendency towards regularity in the timing of the trade cycle in the United States. The results quoted by Sargent overlap with the period analysed here. If his results dismiss periodicity more decisively than ours that may be because we include the most recent American recession in our data. Such evidence of periodicity as we find in the American data, and it is very weak, seems to arise from the experience of the 1970s rather than the 1960s. The main conclusion to be drawn from this comparison, however, is that British experience over this period seems different from American. A much stronger case can be made out for periodicity in the British data. The earlier discussion of the theoretical significance of periodicity suggested that it could vary from time to time and from country to country even if the structure of the economy was similar in every case. This brief comparison of periods and countries is consistent with this suggestion. We turn now to a more detailed consideration of British experience since 1959.

PERIODICITY IN QUARTERLY INDICATOR SERIES

In this section regression models will be estimated in various forms using quarterly data for a number of economic variables. No special significance should be attached to a quarterly, annual or other division of time. The theories discussed in an earlier part of this study make no reference to particular time intervals. They could just as well have been expressed in continuous time, and perhaps it is best to consider the difference equations which are estimated as being approximations to a model of continuous change.

Quarterly observations provide four times as many data points as do annual observations. It may seem that this represents a very great advantage, since all the conclusions that can be drawn about periodicity must be accompanied by a warning of the difficulty of extracting any information from the limited data set available. One might suppose monthly or weekly data would be better still. There is some force in this argument, but not as much as there might at first seem to be. So long as the period of observation extends only to twenty-five years there can only be five examples of a five-year cycle however fine the divisions into which time is divided. Moreover, some quarterly series contain a significant element of interpolation and some degrees of freedom have been used up in the prior adjustment for seasonality.

Some initial results were obtained using six of the CSO quarterly cyclical indicator series. These form a convenient data source, in that the CSO has extracted their trend components in order to clarify the cyclical pattern. But it must be remembered in interpreting the results that the trend-extraction procedure, which uses a five-year moving average, will influence the estimates obtained by any form of regression analysis. Further results, described below, which use alternative methods of trend extraction, suggest that in this case the main features of the results based on the CSO cyclical indicators are quite robust.

Table 4.4 shows the results of fitting second-order autoregression models to the six data series. Half the equations in that table would not generate cycles at all, whilst for two of the others the period of the

Table 4.4. *CSO cyclical indicators: regressions without error models*

$y = ay_{-1} + by_{-2} + c + u$ *(standard errors in parentheses)*

	$\hat{a}$	$\hat{b}$	Implied period of cycles (in quarters)
GDP			
(Output estimate)	0.88	−0.08	—
	(0.10)	(0.10)	
Unemployment	1.81	−0.94	17
	(0.04)	(0.04)	
Index of manufacturing	0.95	−0.16	—
production	(0.10)	(0.10)	
CBI capacity	1.37	−0.56	15
utilisation indicator	(0.09)	(0.09)	
Manufacturers' stocks	1.59	−0.75	15
	(0.07)	(0.07)	
Fixed investment in	0.73	0.08	—
plant and machinery	(0.10)	(0.10)	

cycles implied by the estimated parameters is shorter than that suggested by direct observations of turning points. Only the equation for unemployment would generate cycles of the expected period and damping.

The finding of periodicity in some series, but not others, is difficult to reconcile with any theory of the trade cycle. Suppose all the six variables used as indicators were jointly determined within a system of behavioural relationships. No matter what the cyclical pattern implied by that interaction, one would expect it to be common to them all (see

Wallis, 1977, for a more formal treatment of this point). To take an extreme example, can there really be a four-year cycle in capacity utilisation, but not in manufacturing output? It is easier to believe that the estimation procedure is at fault.

The earlier discussion of trade-cycle theory may suggest a better method of estimation. It was suggested that periodicity which derived from the interaction of two or more behavioural relationships could be accompanied by a pattern in the observed 'errors' or 'residuals' or 'stochastic shocks' which was not white noise. Measurement error in any of the variables used here might also produce autocorrelated error terms in these equations. In the case of these particular variables it is also possible that the process of trend extraction by means of moving averages will have some similar effect. The equations were therefore reestimated by a more general procedure allowing for both autoregressive and moving-average components in the error terms.

Tables 4.5 and 4.6 show the results when a third-order autoregression

Table 4.5. *Regressions with error models*

$y = ay_{-1} + by_{-2} + cy_{-3} + d + u + eu_{-1} + fu_{-2}$ (*standard errors in parentheses*)

	$\hat{a}$	$\hat{b}$	$\hat{c}$	$\hat{e}$	$\hat{f}$
GDP	1.95	1.13	−0.10	−1.35	0.39
	(0.48)	(0.86)	(0.42)	(0.46)	(0.43)
Unemployment	0.94	0.64	−0.83	0.86	−0.02
	(0.12)	(0.20)	(0.11)	(0.16)	(0.11)
Manufacturing	1.36	−0.15	−0.39	−0.66	−0.12
production	(0.25)	(0.43)	(0.21)	(0.27)	(0.25)
Capacity	2.08	−1.47	0.29	−1.19	0.19
utilisation	(0.08)	(0.13)	(0.06)	(—)	(—)
Stock levels	2.40	−1.99	0.55	−1.18	0.18
	(0.06)	(0.11)	(0.06)	(—)	(—)
Investment	1.40	−0.16	−0.40	−0.97	0.11
	(0.18)	(0.32)	(0.16)	(0.19)	(0.25)

model is estimated for each indicator using the *SMALS* programme with a second-order moving average error model.[4] More plausible models were now estimated for all the six indicators used (although in some cases the standard errors on the coefficients remain large). All imply a cycle of about four to five years with sufficiently light damping for such cycles to be quite regular in response to stochastic shocks. They seem therefore to have identified the common features one would expect to find in the behaviour of variables which are part of an inter-connected dynamic system.

Table 4.6. *Parameters implied by estimates in table 4.5*

$$(1 - \alpha L - \beta L^2)(1 - \gamma L)y \equiv y - ay_{-1} - by_{-2} - cy_{-3}$$

	$\hat{\alpha}$	$\hat{\beta}$	$\hat{\gamma}$	Implied period of cycles (quarters)
GDP	1.839	−0.935	0.107	20
Unemployment	1.813	−0.942	−0.877	17
Manufacturing production	1.783	−0.910	−0.424	17
Capacity utilisation	1.750	−0.894	0.320	16
Stock levels	1.815	−0.924	0.590	19
Investment	1.825	−0.939	−0.428	18

PERIODICITY IN UNEMPLOYMENT AND IN GDP

The results of using the CSO indicator series show that it is possible to estimate autoregression equations for a variety of economic data series which have the same pattern of periodicity and accord well with the earlier results which used annual data. There must remain nevertheless some concern that the properties of the data have been distorted by the trend-extraction procedure used. There was, after all, a celebrated case in the 1960s when a later writer was able to demonstrate that the finding reported in a published article on 'long waves' in data which had been 'smoothed' was *solely* the consequence of that procedure and not at all a characteristic of the raw data (see Fishman, 1969, cited in Harvey, 1981). For the next set of results a quite different approach is adopted to trend extraction.

The appropriate treatment of trends is, as we have seen, really a matter for theoretical as well as statistical consideration. For the present the assumption will be made, although it is not the only possible assumption one could make, that the trends in the series being investigated result from dependence on some other trended variable, or variables, which we are not for the present attempting to identify or to measure. In this case the right way to treat the trend is to extract it by regression as part of the same estimation procedure that measures the frequency and damping of periodicity in the data. The examples given here include trends which are linear, quadratic or even higher-order functions of time.

When dealing with the CSO cyclical indicators it was easier to estimate models of unemployment than of other variables. The same remains true when raw data are used. The results, using unemployment measured in thousands, from 1958 to 1982 are reported in table 4.7. The first regression runs over the whole period and implies a cycle with a period of $4\frac{1}{2}$ years with moderate damping, rather more damping and hence less expectation of regularity in the cyclical pattern than is suggested

Table 4.7. *Autoregression model of unemployment*

$$UN = a + bUN_{-1} + cUN_{-2} + dt + et^2 + ft^3 + gt^4 + D631 + D741 + u/(1 - \alpha L)$$

1958(2) – 1982(4)	b	$\hat{c}$		Implied cycle (quarters)	
	1.713	−0.834		18	
	(0.057)	(0.056)			

	$\hat{a}$	d	$\hat{e}$	f	$\hat{g}$
	64	−3.4	0.17	−0.003	0.002
SE = 24.0	(23)	(2.6)	(0.11)	(0.002)	(0.001)

1958(2) – 1970(4)	b	$\hat{c}$		Implied cycle (quarters)	
	1.473	−0.660		14	
	(0.099)	(0.096)			

	$\hat{a}$	d	$\hat{e}$	f	$\hat{g}$
	86	−0.8	−0.05	0.003	−0.003
SE = 18.8	(27)	(5.1)	(0.37)	(0.010)	(0.009)

1971(1) – 1982(4)	b	$\hat{c}$		Implied cycle (quarters)	
	1.797	−0.931		17	
	(0.065	(0.065)			

	$\hat{a}$	d	$\hat{e}$	f	$\hat{g}$
	14182	−763	15.3	−0.13	0.044
SE = 27.0	(6414)	(344)	(7.0)	(0.06)	(0.020)

by the estimates using the CSO cyclical indicators. A rather complicated trend pattern is also estimated, including a quartic term. No great significance should be attached to this. The overall effect of the polynomial in time is to extract a trend that is initially quite flat but accelerates sharply in the 1970s. Separate results are shown for the two halves of the estimation period. Both suggest periodicity, although it is more pronounced in the estimates for the latter half, which tend to dominate the results for the period as a whole.

Estimating models of total output, GDP, proved somewhat more difficult and those reported here are based on a rather unusual transformation. Instead of estimating the equation

$$y = a + by_{-1} + cy_{-2} + u$$

it was found more satisfactory to estimate

$$\Delta y = d + ey_{-1} + f\Sigma y_{-1} + v$$

This relationship may be understood as an integral control mechanism. That is to say, the growth of output depends not only on its starting position but also on the extent to which it has diverged from its equilibrium value in the past. After differencing it and rearranging terms it can be stated as

$$y = (2 + e + f)y_{-1} - (1 + e)y_{-2} + \Delta v$$

which is identical in form to the second-order difference equations which we have been fitting before, with the important exception of the error term. Some of the results reported for the cyclical indicator series suggest a moving-average error structure approximating to a first difference. This is true, for example, of GDP in table 4.5. The results using 'raw' data for GDP are of the same kind. It would certainly be going too far to say that these results point to an integral control mechanism as the origin of the periodicity in GDP. One has to consider all the indicators together and the results for unemployment do not suggest a moving-average error model at all. If the observed error models result at least in part from measurement error it would not be at all surprising if they differ from one series to another.

The main results, using the average estimate of GDP from 1958(2) to 1982(4) are shown in table 4.8.

Over the complete estimation period the estimates suggest a lightly damped cycle with a period of $5\frac{1}{2}$ years. This conforms quite well with the results derived from the CSO cyclical indicators, although the length of the cycle is a little longer and the damping a little more pronounced. (The coefficient on the level of the variable in the transformed equation corresponds to the coefficient on the second lag in the untransformed equation, minus unity.)

Broadly the same estimates are found using data from the two halves of the estimation period, the 1960s and the 1970s, for the parameters which determine periodicity. The parameters which determine the trend are very different in the two sub-periods and the standard error of the equation is larger in the 1970s than in the 1960s. There is a tendency, consistent with the discussion of a previous section above, for the period of the cycle to be a little longer in the 1970s than in the 1960s: about $5\frac{1}{2}$ years, as against about $4\frac{1}{2}$ years. The damping is a little heavier in the 1970s, which may be consistent with the less regular cyclical behaviour already noted. Nevertheless the similarity of the results for the two halves of the estimation period supports the view that the periodicity shown by the estimates for the twenty-five years is systematic rather than merely accidental.

TESTING LINEARITY

Almost all the relationships estimated in this study involve linear difference equations. Yet in the earlier discussion of the theory of the trade

Table 4.8. *Autoregression model of GDP*

$$\Delta\log y = a + b\log y_{-1} + c\Sigma\log y_{-1} + dt + et^2 + ft^3 + gt^4 + D63(1)$$
$$+ D63(2) + D68(1) + D73(1) + D74(1) + D79(2) + u/(1 - \alpha L)$$

			Implied cycle (quarters)		
1958(2) – 1982(4)	b	$\hat c$			
	−0.126	−0.082	22		
	(0.040)	(0.012)			
	$\hat a$	d	$\hat e$	f	$\hat g$
$SE = 0.0075$	0.182	0.34	0.0003	$0.4(10^{-6})$	$-0.8(10^{-6})$
	(0.182)	(0.05)	(0.0001)	$(0.3(10^{-6}))$	$(0.2(10^{-6}))$
			Implied cycle (quarters)		
1959(1) – 1970(4)	b	$\hat c$			
	−0.102	−0.115	18		
	(0.082)	(0.028)			
	$\hat a$	d	$\hat e$	f	$\hat g$
$SE = 0.0065$	−0.045	0.47	0.0005	$-0.5(10^{-7})$	$-0.1(10^{-5})$
	(0.339)	(0.12)	(0.0001)	$(0.4(10^{-5}))$	$(0.3(10^{-5}))$
			Implied cycle (quarters)		
1971(1) – 1982(4)	b	$\hat c$			
	−0.143	−0.083	22		
	(0.055)	(0.018)			
	$\hat a$	d	$\hat e$	f	$\hat g$
$SE = 0.0082$	−1.7	0.45	−0.0017	$0.2(10^{-4})$	$-0.65(10^{-5})$
	(1.6)	(0.14)	(0.0018)	$(0.2(10^{-4}))$	$(0.53(10^{-5}))$
			Implied cycle (quarters)		
1971(1) – 1982(4)[a]	b	$\hat c$			
	−0.089	−0.078	22		
	(0.052)	(0.012)			
	$\hat a$	d	$\hat e$	f	$\hat g$
$SE = 0.0074$	0.052	0.32	0.0003	$0.7(10^{-7})$	$-0.6(10^{-6})$
	(0.23)	(0.05)	(0.0005)	$(0.3(10^{-6}))$	$(0.2(10^{-6}))$

[a] Omitting 1959(4) – 1960(3); 1964(3) – 1965(1); 1969(1) and (2); 1973(2) – 1973(4); 1979(2) and (3).

cycle the alternative possibility was several times mentioned that the trade cycle could be in effect a 'limit cycle' as described by a non-linear difference equation. Such a system would approximate to a stable linear difference equation when it was remote from equilibrium (and hence be globally stable) but approximate to an unstable linear equation when close to equilibrium (and hence be locally unstable).

The fact that stable linear equations can be estimated using all the observations does not settle the issue. As Blatt (1978) has shown, a limit-cycle model of the kind described might, on average over the whole estimation period, give that impression. There is nevertheless a simple method of distinguishing between the two cases. The sample can be split into two groups of observations, those in which output is close to equilibrium and those in which it is relatively remote.

In the present context the periods in which non-linearity is most likely to be observed are those in which capacity utilisation is exceptionally high and output is rising. If full capacity working places a (non-linear) 'ceiling' on the level of output, as the model in Hicks (1950) for example suggests, then excluding these periods from the estimation would provide an interesting test of non-linearity. No doubt other tests on the same lines could be devised.

Fourteen periods were selected as being those in which supply constraints on the growth of output were most likely to be in operation. They were chosen on the criterion that capacity utilisation was both above average and rising according to the CSO's cyclical indicator series, based on the CBI survey. If there is a significant non-linearity caused by capacity constraints, omitting these observations should reduce the negative coefficient on the level of output, and produce estimates consistent with less damped (or even explosive) cycles in the observations to which the constraint does not apply. The results reported at the foot of table 4.8 are consistent with some non-linearity in the relationship, but the difference between the coefficients of this equation and the first equation in that table estimated with all the observations is not statistically significant.

DISCUSSION OF RESULTS

It could be said that the work reported in this chapter has amounted to describing the same phenomenon again and again in slightly different ways. Right at the beginning of the book attention was drawn to a chart with a rather marked appearance of regularity. That regularity has now been described in many different ways, in terms of turning points, autocorrelations, spectral analysis and autoregressions. But these are little more than alternative ways of making the same point. The appearance of the trade cycle in Britain over the last twenty-five years is unusually, although not uniquely, periodic. This remains a statement about appearances, not a hypothesis about the reasons for those appearances. Periodicity has not been stated as a hypothesis, and no attempt has been made to test it. The reason for this has already been indicated. Periodicity is not a characteristic of data which discriminates between rival theories about economic behaviour. It may be helpful to contrast this study with studies of financial market prices designed to test the hypothesis that the path they follow is a random walk. There hypothesis testing is appropriate because there is a well-defined theory of the working of financial markets which predicts that prices in those markets behave in this way. In that case, but not in the case of periodicity, statistical tests of time-series models may discriminate between theoretical models of economic behaviour.[5]

There is nevertheless real advantage in moving from the inspection of charts to the calculation of summary statistics from the same data and especially to the estimation of autoregressions. It has been demonstrated that a number of data series can be described by second-order difference equations with complex roots. The next stage must be to consider why that is true. In other words we will attempt to 'encompass' an autoregression by a behavioural model.[6] The behavioural model will be designed not just to fit the data, but also to explain why the estimated autoregressions have properties of the kind we have described. That is what is involved in the objective of explaining periodicity, as opposed to describing it in different ways.

Some of the difficulties encountered in the work reported here, and the way those difficulties were surmounted, may be of wider relevance for econometric modelbuilding. Initial estimates using ordinary least squares were very misleading. As a check on other methods of estimation, use was made of turning point observations to identify the rough cycle length one would expect to find in estimated models. In rather the same way information based on turning points could also perhaps be used as a guide to the length of leads or lags between variables which would be acceptable in more complicated models. Use was also made of the expectation that most economic variables share the same cycle. This enabled us to reject a whole set of estimates as mutually inconsistent. In rather the same way, estimation of a variety of models might be improved by cross-equation restrictions. It was found helpful either to incorporate into the estimation procedure a moving-average error model or to transform the data by summation. The results obtained this way were very different from, and more plausible than, those obtained by ordinary least-squares regression. That too may be a finding with wider implications for dynamic modelling of macroeconomic variables.

5

EXPLAINING PERIODICITY

In the preceding chapter a number of autoregressions were estimated which described the cyclical behaviour of the economy. These were presented as, on the one hand, a convenient way of summarising the data and, on the other, as a description of time-series behaviour which could be consistent with a variety of theories about the way the economy works. These autoregressions were fitted to several different variables, but each equation involved only one variable (together with some rather complicated trends and dummy variables). This chapter and Chapter 6 are concerned with relationships that involve two or more variables. The aim is to discover how periodicity may arise from their interactions.

Since almost all the variables which are featured in this study have some cyclical characteristics in common there is a clear risk that direct causation will be ascribed to relationships which are in fact largely accidental. The problem of 'spurious correlation' resulting from common trends is a very familiar one in econometrics. There could be a similar problem arising from a common cycle. This chapter begins with a discussion of the methodological issues this would raise. Some examples are given using data for temperature variation over the year to demonstrate the kind of discrimination between hypotheses we would like to be able to make for output variation over the trade cycle.

The next set of results to be reported uses the same quarterly data for GDP as were used in the last section of Chapter 4. A small set of explanatory variables is used in addition to the trends and dummy variables already encountered. These results suggest some very tentative negative conclusions: that is to say, they suggest that some hypotheses about the origin of periodicity can be tentatively excluded.

METHODOLOGY

In a sufficiently large sample it should be possible to distinguish a true behavioural model from a mere statistical association over a rather regular cycle. The equation to estimate is of the form

$$y = ay_{-1} + by_{-2} + cx_{-1} + u$$

If the cyclical pattern observed in y is solely the result of a lagged response to another variable x then the coefficient b should be insignificant. If, on the other hand, there is no true relationship between x and y, except the experience of a common cycle, then the coefficient c should be insignificant.

The methodology can be demonstrated best with an example. For this we need a data source where the true relationship causing periodicity is not in doubt. The best example of regular exogenous periodicity, as has been remarked before, is seasonality. A second-order difference equation was fitted to monthly observations of temperature for the years 1977 to 1982.

The advantage of using this data series is that we know that it contains a systematic undamped cycle of twelve periods caused by variation in the hours of daylight. There is, however, quite a lot of noise superimposed on the seasonal pattern. The sample was deliberately limited to six years. A data set covering six completed cycles of twelve periods must present something like the same uncertainty as the quarterly economic data sets used elsewhere in this paper, which cover approximately five completed cycles of about twenty periods each.

The simplest cyclical model of all is a second-order autoregression in temperature. The data analysed this way suggested a damped cycle of $13\frac{1}{2}$ months

$$y = 1.265y_{-1} - 0.557y_{-2} + 2.28$$
$$(0.104) \quad (0.104) \quad (0.70)$$

As we have seen, estimates using some economic data also tended to overestimate damping and to be imprecise as to the period of the cycle until error models were added.

Introducing hours of daylight, an absolutely regular seasonal variable, has the effect of removing any trace of an endogenous cycle in *all* the variants tried.

For example

$$y = 0.276y_{-1} + 0.315y_{-2} + 1.660x$$
$$(0.096) \quad (0.088) \quad (0.084)$$

where the coefficients on y lagged are quite large, but do not describe a cycle; or better

$$y = 0.029y_{-1} + 0.065y_{-2} - 0.053x + 1.425x_{-1}$$
$$(0.110) \quad (0.105) \quad (0.308) \quad (0.382)$$

where the lag of temperature behind hours of daylight can be picked up by a lagged independent variable, and lagged values of y drop out altogether.

QUARTERLY MODELS WITH EXOGENOUS VARIABLES

It is generally believed that the path of aggregate demand in Britain and hence, in the short run at least, also the path of output and employment, is powerfully influenced by export demand and by fiscal policy. The univariate models of output described in Chapter 4 were expanded to include three exogenous variables: (the log of) export volume, (the log of) government spending and the average rate of tax.

The role of these variables in the generation of the British trade cycle could be of two rather different kinds. The first possibility is that the output cycle in this country is 'forced' by an independent cycle either in the world economy or in government policy (which in turn might be associated, not very convincingly, with the electoral cycle). The second possibility is that the cycle is generated endogenously through an interaction between private sector demand on the one hand and policy or export competitiveness on the other. Provided the value of the relevant variables in the current quarter is exogenous these regressions can be used to explore hypotheses of either kind. If the inclusion of these variables does not change the characteristics of the cycle implied by the regression estimates this would suggest that neither exports nor fiscal policy plays an essential part in the regular periodicity of the trade cycle, even though they may have other important effects on output throughout the period.

Government spending, in volume terms, includes public consumption and public fixed investment (excluding transactions in land and existing dwellings). The average rate of tax was calculated, at current prices, as the ratio of personal taxes (net of family allowances) plus National Insurance contributions, plus all indirect taxes (net of subsidies) to personal sector income. The results are shown in table 5.1.

In the first equation reported only the levels of the exogenous variables have been included. All three are significant, of the right sign and of plausible magnitude relative to the coefficient on the level of GDP. As compared with the estimates reported in table 4.8, the cycle implied by the coefficients of this equation is rather longer in period, about six years, and rather more heavily damped; indeed, the damping in this case is so heavy that one would expect to find difficulty in discovering the length of the cycle in stochastic simulation.

Equation (2) of table 5.1 is a more general specification including a quartic term in time, some additional dummy variables and also the lagged value of the three exogenous variables. The inclusion of these lagged values removes the constraint that the profile of the response of GDP to these variables needs to be the same in every case. Apart from the small (and statistically insignificant) first coefficient on the tax rate, the signs on all coefficients are correct. The implied cycle, both in terms of period and of damping, is now quite similar to that implied by the equations in table 4.8, which include no exogenous variables at all.

The effects of the exogenous variables on output are necessarily transit-

Table 5.1. *Models with exogenous variables*
(Dependent variable is $\Delta \log y$)

Variable	Coefficient		
	Equation (1)	Equation (2)	Equation (3)
$\log y_{-1}$	−0.298	−0.163	−0.205
	(0.058)	(0.047)	(0.051)
$\Sigma \log y_{-1}$	−0.083	−0.079	−0.078
	(0.016)	(0.012)	(0.013)
$\log ex$	0.163	0.124	0.116
	(0.026)	(0.022)	(0.026)
$\log ex_{-1}$	–	−0.076	−0.052
		(0.028)	(0.032)
$\Sigma \log ex_{-1}$	–	–	−0.017
			(0.015)
$\log g$	0.087	0.061	0.065
	(0.038)	(0.053)	(0.056)
$\log g_{-1}$	–	−0.046	−0.108
		(0.054)	(0.059)
$\Sigma \log g_{-1}$	–	–	0.006
			(0.013)
tax	−0.214	0.031	−0.084
	(0.059)	(0.080)	(0.095)
tax_{-1}	–	−0.104	−0.122
		(0.081)	(0.088)
Σtax_{-1}	–	–	−0.023
			(0.013)
Period of implied cycle (quarters)	24	22	23

Note: All equations also included t, t^2, t^3, $D631$, $D741$ and a constant. Equations (2) and (3) also included t^4, $D632$, $D681$, $D731$, and $D792$. y is gross domestic product; ex is export volume; g is government spending on goods and services and tax is the average rate of tax (for definitions see text).

ory in the specifications of equations (1) and (2). This constraint may be theoretically justified if the cycles in output are interpreted as fluctuations of demand about a trend in capacity which is independent of the exogenous variables. However, it is possible that the trend of capacity is in fact influenced by export performance, by public spending or by taxation. To test this longer-term influence the cumulated sum of each of the exogenous variables was included in equation (3). The additional coefficients are all rather small and ill-determined and the coefficient on the cumulated sum of exports has the wrong sign. The cycle implied by this equation is, in period and in damping, intermediate between those for equations (1) and (2), but closer to the latter.

The first comment must be that the results are very different in the three cases and very sensitive to the exact values of parameters which cannot be estimated in this way with any precision. That said, the dyna-

Table 5.2. *Dynamic multipliers implied by table 5.1*

Quarter	Exports plus 1%	Govt. expenditure plus 1%	Tax rate minus 1 percentage point
0	0.12	0.06	−0.03
1	0.14	0.06	0.05
2	0.15	0.06	0.11
3	0.14	0.05	0.16
4	0.12	0.14	0.18
5	0.10	0.03	0.19
6	0.07	0.01	0.18
7	0.04	–	0.16
8	0.01	−0.01	0.13
9	−0.01	−0.02	0.09
10	−0.03	−0.02	0.05
11	−0.04	−0.02	0.02
12	−0.05	−0.02	−0.01
13	−0.05	−0.02	−0.04
14	−0.05	−0.02	−0.06
15	−0.05	−0.01	−0.06
16	−0.04	−0.01	−0.07
17	−0.04	−0.01	−0.07
18	−0.02	–	−0.06
19	−0.01	–	−0.05
20	–	0.01	−0.04
21	0.01	0.01	−0.02
22	0.02	0.01	−0.01

Note: Effects on GDP (%) calculated from table 5.1 equation (2).

mic multipliers calculated for equation (2) are nevertheless of some interest. They are shown in table 5.2. They suggest a relatively small initial impact of demand on output (which would be consistent with a high marginal import propensity). They give the appearance of '100 per cent crowding out' after two years, but in fact this is just the first crossover point of a cyclical response, and the multipliers become positive again after five or six years. The magnitude of multipliers estimated this way may be quite uncertain, but *any* model which interprets the five-year cycle as inherent in the response of the economy to demand stimuli will imply multipliers with broadly this pattern and time scale. They contrast quite markedly with those, based on the National Institute model, shown in table 5.2 above.

It is not suggested that these equations provide a reliable guide to the behaviour of the economy in response to exports or fiscal policy. The conclusion drawn is the negative one that introducing these exogenous variables does not produce an alternative explanation of the cycle to that derived from the univariate models.

In this sense the results are consistent with the hypothesis that the cycle is inherent in the behaviour of the private sector rather than a reflection of exports or fiscal policy formation. This confirms the observation that neither exports nor indices of fiscal policy show a consistent cyclical pattern over the 1960s and 1970s. It also suggests that there is no *combination* of exports and fiscal policy changes which fits the chronology of the output cycle very well either.

6

THE HISTORY OF THE BRITISH TRADE CYCLE
SINCE 1959

Periodicity has been discussed in Chapters 2 and 3 in relation to simple mathematics and macroeconomic theory. In Chapters 4 and 5 evidence of periodicity has been found in data of various kinds and a methodology has been described for investigating how that periodicity may arise.

The approach adopted in this chapter is somewhat different. It is an attempt to blend an historical account, year by year, of the fluctuations in output with a simple statistical analysis using annual observations. This attempt to write 'econometric history' is perhaps an unusual approach to adopt. Historical writing is generally based on informal judgement whilst econometric relationships are used to interpret the whole data period rather than individual years or data points. But the large number of applied economists who now use estimated models to interpret current events or to make forecasts are in fact using the sort of methodology employed in this chapter all the time. It is a valid use of statistical estimation techniques provided that, as an historian, one never forgets the stochastic nature of the relationships which econometrics can estimate.

This chapter begins with an account of the trade cycle as it appeared at the time. This is based on the commentaries published in the *National Institute Economic Review* continuously since 1959. The advantage of using a single source is consistency over time; the disadvantage is that one source cannot represent the range of opinion amongst commentators, which was at times very wide indeed. Ideas derived from that section and elsewhere in this book are then used to estimate a number of alternative simple models to explain the course of output over twenty-five years. The implications of those models for the explanation of individual years are briefly described. The issues to be addressed may be summed up in two questions. Can a consistent explanation be provided for cyclical movements in the British economy covering the 1970s as well as the 1960s? Is the four- to five-year cycle, which is a feature of both decades, systematic or accidental?

THE CYCLE AND ITS CONTEMPORARY EXPLANATION

We have already made use of the CSO's composite indices of cyclical indicators. Although a close inspection of the series shows that some of the turning points identified in these series are by no means unambiguous, they will be used here as a broad guide to the successive phases of expansion and contraction. The coincident index is reproduced in Chart 1.1 on page 1, together with the CBI index of capacity utilisation which is one of the indicator series used by the CSO[1] as a component of that index. In all there are six troughs and five peaks between 1958 and 1981.

The trough of late 1958

The first *Economic Review*, published in January 1959, recognised that output at the end of the preceding year had 'levelled out or perhaps recovered slightly'. This was described, with characteristic caution, as 'partly due to spontaneous forces and partly due to the measures taken by the Government'. The spontaneous forces included an export recovery, whilst the expansionary measures included the relaxation of hire purchase restrictions. It was not realised at the time that a vigorous recovery was getting under way, but spending on consumer durables was correctly identified as an important component.

The peak in spring 1960

The dating of the downturn is not very clear: the CSO gives March as the turning point, but the CBI index of capacity utilisation suggests some time in the summer. The *Economic Review* of July 1960 again emphasises consumer credit restrictions, which had been reimposed in April, as a major reason for expecting slower growth, but mentions also that exports 'have lost momentum'. It bewails the fact that 'the balance of payments prevents more than a slow and interrupted rate of growth' (see *National Institute Economic Review*, no. 10, July 1960, p. 17). This comment seems typical of the way the cycle was interpreted at that time, by most commentators. It was the result of 'stop-go', an alternation of expansionary and contractionary policies as governments sought vainly to reconcile their objectives for growth with the constraint of the balance of payments.

The trough in the winter of 1962–3

The timing of this turning point may owe something to the exceptionally cold weather at the beginning of 1963. Moreover, consumer spending was depressed in the first quarter in anticipation of the budget. In the *Review* for February 1963 the preceding year was described as 'deceptive' in that output was not growing as fast as it appeared at the time. The upturn of 1963 was correctly predicted, in direction but not in scale, and attributed largely to policy changes, including purchase tax cuts in January and an expansionary budget in April.

The peak at the end of 1964

The *Review* of May 1965 described output as 'at about full capacity' but expected (correctly) that there was still some fall in unemployment to come. The view was also expressed (in the August *Review*) that the first quarter had 'probably marked the end of two years of rapid expansion'. Although the measures taken at the end of 1964, which included a tightening of credit control, had not apparently produced immediate 'deflation', it was expected that their effect would be reinforced by the restrictive budget of 1965. Again the course of the cycle was seen as determined primarily by a sequence of policy actions.

The trough in the summer of 1967

The timing of this turning point is especially obscure. The CSO suggest March, but the CBI series showed a fall in capacity utilisation between June and October. The relation between policy and the cycle also becomes rather less easy to discern and other influences on output seem to become more important. The 1967 budget was broadly neutral, although hire purchase restrictions were eased (and further relaxed in August). The *Review* in August was optimistic about growth, relating that view especially to the prospects for consumption. So far the second cycle of the 1960s might be said to have followed a pattern very similar to that of the first cycle. But in November the attempts to maintain the value of sterling had finally to be abandoned and the devaluation was accompanied by a tightening of credit. The recovery nevertheless continued, although consumer spending was no longer in the lead. The *Review* at the time interpreted the devaluation itself as reflationary and it was correct in expecting exports to grow strongly in 1968.

The peak in the spring of 1969

The turning point is now placed by the CSO in May 1969, but at the time it was obscured by the bringing forward of investment at the end of 1968 (to qualify for the bonus on investment grants). The *Review* was not confident that the peak was passed even in August 1969, and said that 'the pace of economic expansion can be expected to quicken in the remainder of the year'. The budget of the preceding year, 1968, had been very deflationary (because the balance of payments did not seem to be responding adequately to the devaluation). Further measures in the same direction were taken in the budget of 1969. Thus policy was exerting a contractionary influence on output at the time of the downturn, but the response seemed rather more delayed than was typical of the 1960s.

In February 1970 the *Review* included a brief section on the trade cycle (see *National Institute Economic Review*, no. 51, February 1970, pp. 33 and 34) which is of particular interest to the present study. The economy had completed two cycles, from the third quarter of 1958 to the third quarter of 1962, and for the third quarter of 1962 to the third quarter of 1967, which were almost like identical twins. 'But', the Institute commented, 'any attempt to characterise the movement of the British economy in the last two years in terms of a similar cycle runs into difficulties'. These difficulties concerned not only the duration and strength of the upturn but also its composition in terms of expenditure components. We can now see (for example, by inspection of chart 1.1) that the economy was, when that comment was being written, in the course of a third cycle broadly comparable with the two that had preceded it. Nevertheless, subsequent events in the 1970s suggest that the Institute was right in thinking that the nature of the trade cycle was, in some respects at least, being modified. In retrospect, the almost exact recapitulation of events in the two cycles from 1958 to 1967 must have been due in part to mere coincidence.

The trough in early 1972

The turning point is located in the quarter of the 'three-day week', caused by power cuts as a result of the miners' strike. There was also some 'holding off' by consumers in (correct) anticipation of an expansionary budget. The budgets of 1971, and especially 1972, were very expansionary; the government's principal aim at this time was to stimulate the growth of output and it was willing to see the exchange rate fall if necessary to make growth attainable. The *Review* in May 1972 said that 'the stimulus given by the budget seems sufficient to achieve a relatively rapid rate of output growth'. It also recognised that the economy was recovering even before the budget. The May unemployment figure was (correctly) seen as a turning point. The *Review* added 'it suggests in fact that last year's reflationary measures were sufficient to halt the rise in unemployment and that doubts about the effectiveness of Keynesian remedies for unemployment were unfounded' (see *National Institute Economic Review*, no. 60, May 1972, p. 14). Unemployment did indeed continue to fall until the end of the following year.

The peak in summer 1973

The upturn, though vigorous, was relatively short-lived. The growth rate, on the average measure of GDP, was actually over 10 per cent between the first quarters of 1972 and 1973. At the peak in 1973 the pressure of demand may have been higher than at any other time in the period covered by this study. It was also a period of rapid expansion for other major industrial countries, and the synchronisation of the cycle worldwide contributed to the burst of commodity price inflation which followed.

The downturn in the summer of 1973 was not preceded by fiscal deflation. The budget of that year was broadly neutral and the cuts in expenditure announced later in the year, but not effective for some time, cannot have contributed (except perhaps by changing expectations) to the early stages of the downturn and recession which followed. In August 1973 the *Review* was still expecting growth of 3 per cent between 1973 and 1974, when the average estimate now shows a fall of 2 per cent. The *Review* argued (in May 1974) that the downturn was not principally the result of 'overheating' or excess demand in the domestic economy, although it recognised that shortages and bottlenecks had been evident in a few sectors. The reasons given included the surge in commodity prices (which was reinforced so far as British import prices were concerned by a 10 per cent fall in the exchange rate) the oil crisis and the second miners' strike. 'It is clear that this combination of events, particularly the last, has dealt a significant blow to business confidence' (see *National Institute Economic Review*, no. 68, May 1974, p. 14).

The trough in the latter half of 1975

The timing of this upturn is not clear: the CSO picks August 1975, but the CBI capacity utilisation series does not turn until January 1976. The reason for the recovery is also more than usually obscure. Fiscal policy remained deflationary in the 1975 budget, and was only mildly expansionary in 1976.

The Institute *Review* puts rather more emphasis on monetary and financial conditions than before (or since) but does not provide any simple explanation of the recovery. Arithmetically it can be attributed in part to exports, responding to devaluation and world recovery, and in part to a reversal of destocking. The slower rate of inflation (after the end of the threshold agreements) probably contributed to the recovery by reducing the savings ratio.

In December 1976 the Government signed a letter of intent to the International Monetary Fund (IMF) which stopped the fall in the pound but also marked a move to a more cautious economic and fiscal strategy.

Possibly for this reason the recovery hesitated during 1977 and the level of capacity utilisation reported by the CBI Survey fell for nine months. The recovery resumed in 1978 helped by a moderately expansionary budget.

The peak in summer 1979

The recovery of the late 1970s was exceptionally long and slow, and arguably it was never complete. The percentage of firms reporting below capacity working never fell below 51 (compared with 39 per cent in 1973 and 42 per cent in 1969). The reasons for the downturn and the recession which followed have been closely studied (for example, in Artis *et al.*, 1984).

The United Kingdom downturn began earlier than that of the other major industrial countries. It is difficult to attribute the downturn itself to fiscal policy, although the 1981 budget in particular contributed to the depth and duration of the recession which followed. A major factor was the loss of international competitiveness caused by the combination of rapid wage inflation with an unprecedented rise in the exchange rate.

The severity of the recession was not foreseen, or even recognised whilst it was happening. It did not happen as a result simply of the predictable effects of a real appreciation on trade volumes. It may have happened rather because firms revised their longer-term expectations about demand and also faced exceptionally severe financial stringency as real appreciation destroyed their profit margins (see Wren-Lewis, 1984).

The trough of early 1981

As in 1975, the upturn was gradual, and it was difficult to judge its timing or its strength. The reasons for the recovery were also rather obscure. It came before the recovery of world economic activity had gained sufficient momentum to provide an explanation. It was not helped by fiscal expansion, although the reduction in nominal interest rates and the abolition of hire purchase controls could be interpreted as expansionary policy moves. As in 1975, the fall in the rate of inflation may have been an important reason for recovery as, once again, the savings ratio fell.

Contrasts between the 1960s and the 1970s

In the 1960s the popular interpretation, set out clearly in the *Review*, is that the 'stops and starts' were associated with economic policy changes, especially changes in purchase tax and credit restrictions. One could, in the tradition of Phillips' well-known articles of the 1950s, construct mathematical models of control systems which would result in oscillations of the kind observed. With qualifications the same story could be told up until 1972, which saw the most expansionary budget of them all.

The explanation of the more recent past in these terms is not so easy. Fiscal policy did not apparently contribute to either the upturns or the downturns after the early 1970s. Although the United Kingdom moved into rather closer synchronisation with the world cycle, and was presumably influenced by world events like the two oil price 'shocks', the timing does not seem right for world events to provide the sole explanation. Variations in the rate of inflation and in international competitiveness could be important too.

The difficult task is not to explain either the 1960s or the 1970s on their own, it is to provide a consistent account which covers both periods and which explains why a cycle of relatively constant and regular periodicity can be observed from the late 1950s right up to the present day. With this in mind we begin a more formal statistical analysis in the next section.

ANNUAL MODELS OF THE CYCLE

In this section annual data and *OLS* regression are used to estimate the kind of relationships suggested by the historical account given above and the theory outlined in Chapter 3. In contrast to much recent econometric practice the account of the results here proceeds from the most simple to the more elaborate or general. This seems the right order to adopt on this occasion, because interest centres on the way in which a more general model can explain (or 'encompass') a simple one, and in particular how a behavioural model can 'encompass' an autoregression.

The relationships are relatively unsophisticated in estimation methods. Work described elsewhere in this paper demonstrates the importance of alternative treatments of error dynamics when estimating time-series models of the cycle. Here the emphasis is quite different. The aim is to explain the cycle by introducing a range of exogenous (or predetermined) variables. The complex error dynamics of simple time-series models may result from the omission of these variables. With the annual data set used here there is not much scope for additional complexity.

The dependent variable, defining the cycle, is industrial output (the index for total production industries given in *Economic Trends*). This was preferred to GDP partly on the grounds that it is likely to be less subject to measurement error. The cyclical fluctuations with which the study is concerned are concentrated mainly in the industrial sector rather than, for example, in agriculture or public administration. It is worth emphasising that the aim here is to explain those cyclical, and perhaps periodic, fluctuations which are common to the whole economy, so the choice of dependent variable is a matter of convenience rather than conformity with theory.

The estimated equations all included, in addition to the independent variables itemised below, a constant and a time trend. The time trend was included because the aim of the exercise is specifically to explain cyclical fluctuations rather than the average growth rate of the economy over the period as a whole. The difficulties of separating cycle and trend have been discussed in Chapter 3 above.

World industrial output

In all the results reported a significant determinant of output in this country is the level of industrial output in the OECD area as a whole in the same year. It was decided that this was the best way of modelling those trends and fluctuations which are common to the industrial world as a whole rather than peculiar to Britain. The slower growth rate of the 1970s compared with the 1960s is one feature of the data which is 'explained' in this way. Some of the effects of world oil and commodity price movements are also subsumed into the effects of changes in world output. Thus, the study does not seek to distinguish the effects of world output in this country from the effects of other influences on both world output and output in this country. The aim is rather to set on one side all fluctuations which are common to the whole industrial world in order to concentrate on peculiarly British history. Including world industrial output amongst the independent variables seems the most convenient way of doing this.

Competitiveness

The index used is the IMF series for relative unit labour costs (extrapolated back before 1963 using data for wage costs in four major countries). This variable is included to capture the effect of relative prices on the volume of imports and exports but also the effect of relative profit margins on production decisions or cash flow. The most important changes in this variable take place at the time of the 1967 devaluation, the sterling crises of 1972 and 1976, and (especially) the appreciation of sterling in 1979 and 1980. The index is treated as exogenous since none of these

major movements can be explained by the contemporaneous movement
of industrial production in this country.

Fiscal policy

The 'stance' of fiscal policy can be measured in many different ways.
The measure used for this study is the 'weighted and cyclically adjusted'
fiscal deficit. The method of weighting tax and expenditure changes,
and the method of cyclical adjustment, are both described in an article
by D. Savage in the *Review* for February 1982. A data series for fiscal
years from 1960/1 to 1982/3 is given in the *Review* for February 1984
(see *National Institute Economic Review*, no. 107, February 1984, p. 80).
No inflation adjustment was made to the deficit but the rate of inflation
is included in the estimated relationships as a separate variable (on the
grounds that the effect of inflation on output will not be fully captured
by making an adjustment to the variable representing fiscal policy). The
weights applied to the various tax and spending changes are strictly
applicable to GDP rather than to industrial output. Moreover the method
of calculation leaves open the question of how quickly fiscal policy affects
output. In practice it was found that lagged values of the fiscal policy
variable were significant whilst current values were not. It is doubtful
however, whether the *current* value of fiscal indicators can be regarded
as exogenous in an equation explaining output. For that to be true the
cyclical correction must be exactly right and moreover decisions about
fiscal policy must not be influenced by the current output level. In an
annual model this last assumption may well be invalid, although it would
be difficult to argue that fiscal policy since 1959 has been consistently
used for output stabilisation. In any case, none of the equations reported
use the current fiscal indicator. Indeed, quite a long lag is assumed,
such that, for example, fiscal policy in the financial year 1960/1 first
affects output in the calendar year 1962.[2]

Monetary policy

The indicator used is the nominal interest rate (the London clearing
banks' rate for seven-day deposits). For most of the period short-term
interest rates were dominated by the actions of the monetary authorities
in setting bank rate or the Minimum Lending Rate. (Although monetary
targets were set for part of the period there was no direct instrument
to control the money supply or domestic credit expansion.) During the
1960s in particular, interest rate changes were almost always reinforced
by changes in hire purchase regulations or in the ceilings on bank lending
to the private sector. No attempt has been made to isolate these different

aspects of monetary policy or assess the relative effectiveness of different instruments. After some experimentation it was decided to use the inverse of the interest rate in the regressions. This means that a change of 1 percentage point in the rate has a more powerful effect on output when the initial rate is low, as it typically was in the 1960s, than when it is high, as it typically was in the 1970s. This particular transformation could perhaps be justified in terms of the relationship between interest rates and bond prices but in that case presumably the long-term rate would be more appropriate than the seven-day rate. No attempt has been made to estimate the effects of *real* interest rates, but inflation is included in some of the estimated equations as an additional explanatory variable. There are arguments, related to credit availability, which suggest that the nominal interest rate may work better as an index of the stringency of financial markets than does any feasible calculation of real rates. It cannot be argued that current nominal interest rates are exogenous. On the contrary, the results reported include equations for interest rates in which they are influenced by the current value of output. Fortunately, however, one can appeal to the property common to most models of the British economy that interest rates affect output only after a significant lag. Thus the current value of interest rates has not been included as a determinant of output in any of the equations estimated.

Inflation

Two reasons have already been given for including the rate of inflation in the relationships that explain output fluctuations, but they would tend to cancel each other out. Other things being equal, higher inflation implies lower real interest rates, thus raising output, but it also implies a smaller 'inflation-adjusted' fiscal deficit, thus reducing output. In fact, it is widely believed that the effect of inflation (or at least of accelerating inflation) on output is powerful and adverse. The theoretical basis for the presumption is not often clearly stated but a book of this kind is not the best place to rectify that weakness. One can point to the effect of inflation on uncertainty or, more concretely, at its effect on expectations of future policy moves by the monetary or fiscal authorities. One can also suppose that inflation leads to misperceptions of real income or to loss of economic efficiency. None of these theoretical arguments carries great conviction on its own, but the informal account of the cycle already given does point to variations in the rate of inflation as a possible explanation of several of the more recent cyclical turning points. The results reported below confirm this. As with nominal interest rates, the question of exogeneity arises also for the use of the current rate of inflation in explaining output. The approach adopted is parallel. It is found that output *does* affect inflation in the current period, but that the effect in the reverse direction from inflation to output is lagged.

Lagged values of output

Special interest attaches in this study to the dynamic form of the equations which determine output. The theoretical reasons for expecting 'persistence' even if expectations are rational have been extensively studied in recent years. Moreover, in this study expectations are not assumed to be rational and are not explicitly modelled. It is possible therefore that the persistence of output fluctuations may reflect expectations which are adaptive rather than rational as well as costs of adjusting output or other rigidities. Chapter 3 includes some considerations of the theoretical basis for periodicity in output fluctuations. If this occurs it can be approximated by a second-order autoregressive model. In the results reported below the value of output lagged two years was included on several occasions to allow for this possibility.

THE RESULTS

The estimated equations are set out in table 6.1. They were all fitted to annual data from 1959 to 1983 inclusive using ordinary least squares regression. They are presented in what appears after the event to be the logical sequence, not the order in which they were actually estimated (neither are all the equations estimated of sufficient interest to report).

Equation (1) The first equation reported simply fits a quadratic time trend to the output data. The negative coefficient on t^2 indicates as expected that the growth rate of output was slowing down. The residuals from this equation are tabulated in table 6.2. They correspond well with the chronology of the cycle discussed earlier in this chapter. Their tendency to periodicity is confirmed by the residual correlogram which is markedly negative at two- and three-year lags, but markedly positive at five.

Equation (2) The next equation abandons higher-order trends in favour of the world output variable. For the reasons given above this seemed a better way of dealing with the trend component of British output growth. The equation also fits much better. Some cyclical variation is also eliminated, especially that in the 1970s associated with the first OPEC price increase. Nevertheless, the residuals are still periodic, as can be seen from table 6.2 or the residual correlogram. This suggests that the periodicity of the British cycle is not just a reflection of periodicity in the world cycle.

Equation (3) is reported only to make clear that introducing first-order

Table 6.1. *Estimated equations using industrial production*
Annual data, 't' values in parentheses

(1) $y = 4.0 + 0.0493t - 0.0010t^2$
      (12.1)   (7.3)
      $R^2 = 0.964$ $LM = 13.5$
Residual correlogram: 0.25, −0.60, −0.53, 0.11, 0.47, 0.08

(2) $y = 1.8 - 0.0056t + 0.633w$
      (2.6)   (12.1)
      $R^2 = 0.983$ $LM = 9.5$
Residual correlogram: 0.14, −0.54, −0.43, 0.26, 0.25, −0.16

(3) $y = 1.6 - 0.0039t + 0.139y_{-1} + 0.704w - 0.173w_{-1}$
      (1.4)   (0.6)   (5.8)   (0.9)
      $R^2 = 0.984$ $LM = 11.3$
Residual correlogram: 0.02, −0.50, −0.35, 0.33, 0.19, −0.23

(4) $y = 1.2 + 0.0025t + 0.286y_{-1} + 0.615w - 0.154w_{-1} + 0.156\ 1/r_{-1}$
      (0.9)   (1.4)   (5.3)   (0.9)   (2.4)
      $R^2 = 0.988$ $LM = 4.3$
Residual correlogram: 0.08, −0.27, −0.33, −0.07, −0.01, −0.16

(5) $1/r = 3.3 - 0.697y - 0.616y_{-1} + 0.64w - 0.0039t + 0.77\ 1/ru + 0.20\ 1/i - 0.38\ 1/iw$
      (1.2)   (1.5)   (1.2)   (0.5)   (2.1)   (2.4)   (1.1)
      $R^2 = 0.826$ $LM = 8.0$

(6) $y = 2.4 - 0.0031t + 0.195y_{-1} - 0.393y_{-2} + 0.692w$
      (1.6)   (1.5)   (3.7)   (8.4)
      $R^2 = 0.990$ $LM = 0.8$

(7) $y = 2.1 - 0.0025t + 0.256y_{-1} - 0.327y_{-2} + 0.636w + 0.091\ 1/r_{-1}$
      (1.3)   (1.9)   (2.9)   (7.2)   (1.5)
      $R^2 = 0.991$ $LM = 0.4$

(8) $y = 1.2 + 0.0059t + 0.479y_{-1} + 0.213y_{-2} + 0.437w - 0.300w_{-1} + 0.006z_{-1} - 0.119c$
      (3.0)   (5.2)   (2.1)   (8.5)   (3.5)   (3.3)   (6.3)
      $+ 0.152\ 1/r_{-1} - 0.0060i_{-1} + 0.0022i_{-2}$
      (4.9)   (6.3)   (3.4)
      $R^2 = 0.999$ LM (not reported)

(9) $i = -239 + 0.42t + 0.38i_{-1} + 12.8y + 83.4y_{-1} - 44.3w + 7.5\ 1/r + 1.4z$
      (1.3)   (2.5)   (0.5)   (4.9)   (2.2)   (0.9)   (3.6)
      $R^2 = 0.905$ $LM = 1.5$

(10) $i = -170 + 0.31t + 0.33i_{-1} + 23.3y + 52.4y_{-1} - 40.0w + 7.5\ 1/r + 0.9z + 0.89iw$
      (1.2)   (2.5)   (1.1)   (3.1)   (2.5)   (1.1)   (2.6)   (3.1)
      $R^2 = 0.941$ $LM = 3.4$

Definitions: y = industrial output (log of); w = world industrial output (log of); r = short-term interest rate; ru = US short-term interest rate; i = rate of inflation (%, p.a.); iw = world rate of inflation (%, p.a.); z = index of fiscal policy; c = index of competitiveness (log of)

lags on their own does not eliminate the periodicity. Neither does it improve the fit of the equation.

Table 6.2. *Scaled residuals from estimated equations of table 6.1*

	(1)	(2)	(4)	(6)	(8)
1959	0.3	−0.4	0.3	0.1	0.0
1960	1.1	1.3	0.4	1.0	−0.2
1961	−0.0	0.7	0.7	0.3	1.0
1962	−1.0	−0.6	−0.2	−0.2	−0.5
1963	−1.1	−1.2	−1.3	−1.3	−1.3
1964	0.3	0.8	−0.4	0.6	0.3
1965	0.2	0.2	−0.1	−0.7	0.9
1966	−0.3	−0.8	−0.5	−0.8	0.0
1967	−1.0	−1.1	−0.7	−1.0	−1.6
1968	0.5	0.8	1.4	1.3	0.4
1969	0.8	0.1	0.4	−0.7	0.6
1970	0.2	0.2	0.6	0.5	1.3
1971	−0.6	−0.2	−0.1	0.6	0.8
1972	−0.6	−1.0	−1.4	−0.6	−0.9
1973	1.6	0.5	0.4	0.4	0.5
1974	0.5	−0.2	0.0	−1.1	−1.5
1975	−1.7	−0.1	0.3	1.3	−0.1
1976	−1.0	−0.8	−0.6	0.3	0.5
1977	0.3	0.9	1.3	0.4	−0.3
1978	1.1	1.3	0.5	0.7	0.3
1979	2.1	1.8	1.3	1.9	−0.5
1980	−0.2	−0.9	−1.4	−1.3	−0.3
1981	−1.4	−2.4	−2.1	−1.6	0.0
1982	−0.8	−0.0	0.6	0.1	0.9
1983	0.4	0.9	0.6	−0.1	−0.4

Equation (4), which adds the nominal interest rate, is a significant improvement. As table 6.2 shows, the cycles of the 1960s are now 'explained' and largely disappear from the residuals.

Equation (5) is an equation for the nominal interest rate, estimated for convenience with the inverse as the dependent variable. It has much in common with the specification used by Jane Darby (1984) in a recent note in the *Review* and is best understood as the authorities' 'reaction function'. The main determinants of British interest rate movements are overseas interest rates and the British rate of inflation. (The specification is designed so as to be relevant to either a fixed or a floating exchange rate regime). There is also an effect from the level of output in this country relative to the output of other industrial countries. It is this last term which is of most interest in the present context. Can the periodic element in the cycle be explained by substituting equation (5) into equation (4)? In other words, is the cycle caused by the interaction of output and interest rates (where interest rates are viewed as an index of monetary policy)? The equation for output derived in this way would be

$$y = 0.177y_{-1} - 0.096y_{-2} + \dots$$

This autoregression does indeed imply a periodic cycle with a period of about $4\frac{1}{2}$ to 5 years. However, the coefficient on y_{-2} is very low even for annual data, so the cycles generated by this autoregression would be very damped. Autoregressions in which the damping is heavy will not produce cycles which are perceptibly periodic in response to a random noise input. Thus the interaction between output and interest rates, whilst it may have some role to play in generating cycles cannot, if these estimates are reliable, provide the whole explanation.

Equation (6) provides for comparison a directly estimated second-order autoregression for output in which world output is the only exogenous variable added to the lagged output terms. The coefficient on output lagged two years is 0.39, which is much larger than the coefficient of 0.096 calculated from the two preceding equations. (Indeed with annual data 0.39 is quite a high coefficient, corresponding to about 0.8 for quarterly data.) The period of the implied cycle is again about $4\frac{1}{2}$ years and, as one would expect, the residuals, tabulated in table 6.2, give no suggestion of a regular cycle.

Equation (7) confirms that interest rates do not do much to explain the appearance of periodicity. The test applied here is similar to that used in a different context (seasonality) in Chapter 5. The variable under examination, in this case the lagged value of the inverse of the short-term interest rate, is introduced alongside the autoregressive terms in output which define the cycle. The result shows that the cycle is *not* eliminated (although the coefficient y_{-2} is slightly reduced). Thus the time path for output will, according to this equation, have very much the same cyclical characteristics whether interest rates are free to respond or whether they are held fixed.

Equation (8) After a good deal of experimentation this equation was chosen as providing probably the most comprehensive explanation of the output cycle one could expect to obtain from annual observations. As well as the variables already mentioned there are indices of fiscal policy, competitiveness and inflation. Nearly half the degrees of freedom available have been used up and the residuals are small relative to the measurement error one would expect for industrial output. As the final column of table 6.2 shows, the scaled residuals are highest in 1963, 1967 and 1974. The first of these may be the result of the exceptionally cold weather and the third of the miners' strike. One of the more satisfactory features of the equation is its ability to track the period since the mid-1970s so closely. The other residual series shown in the table all fail to explain the peak of activity in 1979 and the depth of the 1980–1 recession. The coefficients in this equation are all of the expected sign and at least broadly of the expected order of magnitude (for an account of the determination of industrial output, but not necessarily of GDP).

World output: the movement corresponding to a 1 percentage change is nearly ½ both in the short run and in the long run. *Fiscal policy*: if the weighted and cyclical-adjusted deficit increased by 1 per cent of GDP, industrial output rises by a little over ½ per cent after nearly a year and by more than 1 per cent eventually. *Competitiveness*: A rise of 10 per cent in relative unit labour costs has an immediate effect of about 1 per cent on output and a long-term effect of about 3 per cent. *Monetary policy*: A rise of 1 percentage point in interest rates, assuming an initial level of 10 per cent will cut output about a year later by about 1½ per cent, taking the level of competitiveness as unchanged. Again the long-term effect (suppressing the feedback from output to interest rates) would be substantially greater. *Inflation*: A rise in the rate of inflation of a percentage point will, after a year's delay, reduce output by about ½ per cent. Thereafter the effect may wear away for a time (perhaps because persistent inflation is not as damaging as unexpected inflation) but the ultimate effect (suppressing any feedback) is about 1½ per cent.

Equation (9) seeks to explain the rate of inflation, although clearly that task cannot be very seriously addressed here and merits a research project of its own. As one would expect, the lagged value of inflation plays an important role, although a coefficient as low as 0.38 does not seem to accord well with theories of expectations and the 'augmented Phillips Curve.' Output, and especially output lagged one year, also seems important. The mechanism underlying this effect could work either through the labour market or, since the 1970s, through the foreign exchange market. The negative effect of world output could be interpreted in two ways; either it is acting as a proxy for the trend of supply potential in this country or it has a real effect on inflation through the foreign exchange market. The effects of interest rates and, especially, of fiscal policy, suggest that expansionary policy moves act directly and quickly on inflation even though, as we have seen, they may only act with a lag on the level of industrial output. Again one suspects that the foreign exchange market may be involved.

Equation (10) is an alternative equation for inflation introducing the world inflation rate as an explanatory variable. This parallels the use of world variables in the output (and interest rate) equations and should not necessarily be interpreted as meaning that world inflation causes inflation in this country. It may be that world inflation is acting as a 'proxy' for shifts in behaviour which occurred in this country and others at about the same time. (Greater union militancy in the 1970s would be an explanation of this kind.) The short-run coefficient is less than unity but, allowing for the lagged dependent variable, the long-run coefficient would be 1.3. A different specification which omitted the interest rate and fiscal policy variables as well as the lagged output level resulted in a much higher coefficient on world inflation: 1.4 in the short run and 2.7 in the long run. This could be interpreted as meaning that this country was for some reason much more sensitive than most other industrial countries to the forces which accelerated inflation in the 1970s.

It cannot be said that any of these equations produce a very satisfactory account of inflation but they are probably correct in suggesting that there is some relationship between output and inflation and that this is important to the explanation of the cyclical movements in output. The next stage therefore is to substitute the inflation equations into the equation for output. Equation (9) can be substituted into equation (8) to eliminate the term in inflation, and equation (5) used to eliminate the term in the nominal rate of interest. The equation for output derived this way would be

$$y = 0.327y_{-1} - 0.353y_{-2} + \ldots$$

This autoregression again implies a periodic cycle with a period of nearly five years and the damping is only moderate. Indeed this autoregression would not be very different in its characteristics from that directly estimated as equation (6). On the other hand, using equation (10) in place of equation (9) would produce a rather different autoregression

$$y = 0.264y_{-1} - 0.167y_{-2}$$

which implies a cycle with a period a little over five years and heavier damping. In other words, if one uses world inflation as part of the explanation of inflation in this country then the importance of systematic or endogenous periodicity in the resulting model for the British trade cycle is reduced, although not altogether eliminated. The case for including some effect from world inflation in any explanation of British inflation must be very strong, if only because the commodity price increases of 1972 and the oil price increases of 1973 and 1979 cannot possibly be interpreted as the result of movements in any domestic variables in this country.

STOCKS AND THE CYCLE

In the discussion of the theory of the trade cycle in Chapter 3 a brief account was given of the multiplier–accelerator models developed in the 1940s and 1950s. These were quite different in conception from the ideas used in this econometric history, or indeed in the contemporary account of events derived from back numbers of the Institute's *Economic Review*. Most commentators have used, and still use, movements in stocks and fixed investment as one element in their account of trade-cycle behaviour. But, as we have seen, the explanation offered of major turning points is not generally of this kind. It is of some interest nevertheless to investigate how well the events of the last twenty-five years could be explained by a model which emphasised the stock cycle to the exclusion of almost everything else.

Data on the total volume of stocks at the end of each year was extracted from successive numbers of the Blue Book. This variable (as a logarithm) was used first in a very simple relationship to explain (the logarithm of) output. World output and time were the only other variables included. The coefficient on stocks was of the right sign, but not very significant. The results are reported as equation (1) of table 6.3.

Table 6.3. *Estimated equations for an inventory cycle*
Standard errors in parentheses

(1) $y = 1.68 - 0.0042t + 0.34y_{-1} + 0.67w - 0.37s_{-1}$
    (0.35) (0.0022) (0.24)   (0.10) (0.20)
    $R^2 = 0.986$ $LM = 3.6$
(2) $s = 0.49 - 0.0001t + 0.32s_{-1} + 0.73y_{-1}$
    (0.47) (0.0027) (0.29)   (0.31)
    $R^2 = 0.980$ $LM = 4.6$
(3) $y = 2.57 - 0.0032t + 0.11y_{-1} - 0.45y_{-2} + 0.69w + 0.13s_{-1}$
    (0.43) (0.0019) (0.22)   (0.15)   (0.08) (0.24)
    $R^2 = 0.990$ $LM = 0.9$

Definitions: as table 6.1, but s = volume of total stocks (log of).

Equation (2) of the same table explains the level of stocks as a process of adjustment towards a desired relationship with output. Again the coefficients are of the right sign although not very significant. Combining these two equations would produce a second-order difference equation for output

$$y = 0.66y_{-1} - 0.38y_{-2} \ldots$$

In terms of damping this is not very different from the directly estimated second-order difference equation reported as equation (6) of table 6.1. The period, however, is rather longer, over six years, which does not accord well with what we know about turning points.

It should be clear, however, from what has gone before that the finding of a bivariate relationship of this kind between two cyclical variables does not amount to strong evidence that these two variables actually interact to cause the periodicity that the equation implies. In fact the third equation of table 6.3 suggests that they do not. The value of output lagged two periods is included in the regression as well as the level of stocks. The result is a second-order difference equation in output which on its own explains (or describes) the periodicity of the cycle. The term in stocks is insignificant and of the wrong sign.

This result does not exclude the possibility that stocks play some part in the generation of the periodic cycles we observe. As with interest rates it is possible that some role could be found for them in a more general model like that of equation (8) in table 6.1 All one can say is that a stockbuilding accelerator model on its own does not, on the basis of this experiment, look promising as an explanation of the British trade cycle in the 1960s and 1970s.

This perhaps accords well with historical intuition. Nothing really out of the ordinary has been observed about the behaviour of stocks in this country over this period as compared with other countries or other periods. The behaviour of interest rates, and especially of inflation, was perhaps rather unusual. It should not be so surprising therefore if that unusual behaviour had something to do with the unusual regularity of the trade cycles we observe.

To give a fair run to one important strand in trade-cycle theory, the analysis of this section should be repeated for fixed investment. It should be possible, in principle, to model the interaction of the level of output and the level of fixed capital in a way which parallels the treatment of output and stocks. Since the cyclical behaviour of stockbuilding and of (private sector, non-dwelling) fixed investment is rather similar, at least with regard to timing, rather similar results might be obtained. To make the investigation worthwhile, however, one would need to have a direct measure of the capital stock, a measure based on actual observation of depreciation and scrapping, not an artificial construct based on assumptions about typical asset lives. It is very likely that scrapping actually varies over the cycle, although no allowance is made for this in calculating the official capital stock series. For this reason any investigation directed specifically at the cyclical relationship between output and the capital stock would be unsatisfactory and incomplete.

AN ECONOMETRIC HISTORY

At the risk of repetition the story of the twenty-five year period will be retold twice. The first account will be based on a second-order autoregression in industrial output in Britain with world output as an additional explanatory variable, that is on equation (6) of table 6.1 described above. That story is summarised by table 6.4.

The strong growth in output in 1960 is partly explained by the world output cycle which roughly coincided with our own at this point. The slow growth of the next two years was a cyclical reaction caused by some unspecified 'negative feedback' in the British economy. This cyclical effect was spent by 1963 and the upturn was then reinforced by some unspecified boost to output (a 'residual' in the equation) between 1963 and 1964. The pattern then repeated itself in the middle years of the decade with the 'negative feedback' slowing growth down to 1 per cent

Table 6.4. *The path of output as explained by equation (6) of table 6.1*

| Year | Change in output due to (percentage points) | | | Actual |
	World output	Lagged UK output	Residual	
1960	4	1	+2	7
1	2	−1	−1	—
2	5	−3	−2	1
3	6	—	−2	3
4	5	—	+3	8
5	5	—	−2	3
6	5	−3	—	2
7	2	−1	—	1
8	4	−1	+4	7
9	6	1	−3	3
70	1	−2	+2	—
1	1	−1	—	—
2	4	—	−2	2
3	7	1	+2	9
4	—	1	−3	−2
5	−6	−4	+4	−6
6	6	−1	−2	3
7	2	3	—	5
8	3	—	+1	3
9	4	−1	+2	4
80	−1	—	−5	−7
1	—	−3	−1	−4
2	−3	2	+3	2
3	3	2	−1	3

Note: Figures do not add because of rounding and the exclusion of the time trend.

a year. By 1968 the economy was ready for another burst of growth which was partly caused by the world output cycle but partly by another unspecified 'residual' effect. The reaction set in in 1970 and 1971.

In the 1970s too some of the more interesting episodes are incompletely explained. The 1973 boom was partly a reflection of world conditions, but not all of it is explained. By contrast the 1975 recession is over-explained by world conditions, together with a cyclical reaction after the 'overshooting' of output two years previously. From 1976 to 1979 the equation fits quite well. In 1977 in particular the continuing cyclical upturn can be explained as a reaction from the depth of the preceding recession. No adequate account, however, can be given in this framework for the sharp downturn in 1980 which preceded the worst of the world recession and which did not follow a period of exceptionally rapid growth in this country. Moreover, the recovery from the recession in 1982 is only partly explicable by 'spontaneous cyclical forces' since these could not have been sufficiently powerful to offset the continuing world recession.

To sum up, the autoregression model fails to account for some of the most interesting cyclical features of history. The 'stop-go' pattern of the 1960s is partly explained but there are also unexplained 'residual' boosts to output in all the years of strong upswing. The especially interesting pattern of slump and recovery in the early 1980s remains largely unexplained.

The second account, based on equation (8) of table 6.1 is much more comprehensive, and it is documented in table 6.5. The effect of lagged output is now reinforcing (a 'positive' rather than a 'negative' feedback) although this is commonly offset by induced changes in either interest

Table 6.5. *The path of output as explained by equation (8) of table 6.1*

Year	Change in output due to (percentage points)							
	World output	Lagged UK output	Competitiveness	Interest rates	Inflation	Fiscal policy	Residual	Actual
1960	—	2	—	3	2	—	—	7
1	—	4	−1	−3	—	—	1	—
2	2	1	—	−1	−1	—	−1	1
3	2	—	—	1	−1	—	−1	3
4	1	1	—	2	1	—	1	8
5	1	4	—	−3	−1	1	—	3
6	1	3	—	−1	−1	—	−1	2
7	−1	2	1	—	1	−1	−1	1
8	2	—	2	—	1	—	1	7
9	2	3	—	−1	−1	—	—	3
70	−1	2	—	—	—	−1	1	—
1	−1	1	—	—	−1	−1	—	—
2	3	—	—	1	−2	1	−1	2
3	3	1	1	—	1	1	1	9
4	−3	4	—	−2	−1	1	−1	−2
5	−4	1	−1	—	−4	1	1	−6
6	6	−3	1	—	−4	1	1	3
7	−1	1	—	—	7	−1	−1	5
8	1	3	−1	1	−2	−1	1	3
9	2	2	−2	−1	5	−1	−1	4
80	−2	2	−3	−1	−5	—	—	−7
1	—	−2	—	—	−2	—	—	−4
2	−2	−3	—	—	5	—	1	2
3	4	—	1	—	1	−1	−1	3

Note: Figures do not add because of rounding and the exclusion of the time trend.

rates or inflation. The effect of world output is rather weaker in this equation compared to the previous one, and tends to 'overshoot'.

The 1960 boom was the result of lower inflation and also lower interest rates in the preceding year. The momentum was not continued in 1961 because interest rates were raised. In 1962 and 1963 there was a positive effect from the world output cycle which helped the early stages of upturn in the latter year. The strength of the boom in 1964, however, is again (as was that in 1960) due to lower interest rates and inflation in the preceding year. The downturn of 1965 was due to high interest rates and inflation which overcame the momentum built up at the peak of the boom. The upswing of 1968 was quite different in character, being initiated partly by growth in the rest of the world, but also by the gain in competitiveness following the 1967 devaluation. The simultaneous tightening of fiscal policy was not enough to prevent a substantial cyclical upturn. Again in 1969 the momentum of output would have prolonged the upswing had interest rates and inflation not risen. By 1970 a downturn in world output and resumed fiscal deflation were enough to stop output growth altogether.

The path of output in 1972 and 1973 is not perfectly captured by the equation but, taking the two years together, the boom is attributed mainly to world output growth reinforced by domestic fiscal policy. In the downturn of 1974 we again see the inertia of output overcome by monetary policy and inflation, reinforced this time by the halt to growth in the world economy. In 1975 it was mainly inflation that prolonged and deepened the recession. The inflation of this period is explained in equation (9) as domestic in origin but by equation (10) as the result of an inflationary impulse coming from the world economy.

The economy recovered in 1976, despite the continuing effects of high inflation, thanks to a powerful stimulus from the world output cycle and an improvement in cost competitiveness after the sterling crisis of that year. A slowing down of inflation, and the weakening effect on output of the inflation that remained, contributed to continued expansion in 1977, despite a reversal of fiscal policy (at the time of the IMF Letter of Intent). By 1978 the pound was strong again and interest rates had fallen, but these two forces roughly balanced each other in their effect on output. Growth was relatively slow because inflation had been rising again. Success in curbing inflation in 1978, during the early stages of an incomes policy not explained by either equation (9) or equation (10), helped growth in 1979, although by then the rise in sterling and tighter monetary policy were working in the opposite direction.

The path of output since 1980 is explained very fully by this equation. What happened in 1980 was partly due to the first faltering of the world output cycle, partly to the exceptionally sharp loss of competitiveness, but also (to a rather surprising extent) to the acceleration of inflation because incomes policy broke down (and indirect taxes were raised) in the preceding year. The momentum of this fall in output carried the recession on into 1981, despite a 'false dawn' in the world output cycle. The British recovery in 1982, despite deepening recession elsewhere, was due to the sharp slowing down in inflation. The depressing effect of a tight fiscal policy was not felt until 1983 and then served only to weaken the recovery brought about by the upswing in world economic activity and the fall of the pound.

This brings the story almost up to date. This historical account is certainly more satisfactory than the one based on a 'spontaneous' cycle and the contemporary movements in world activity alone. Nevertheless, it raises some problems. Partly what has been done is to transfer the uncertainty from the explanation of output to the explanation of inflation. If we were better able to explain the variation in the inflation rate we would be more confident that we had a good historical account of output fluctuations. It is possible, moreover, that the various factors which influenced inflation (the oil price shocks for example or incomes policy phases) also had direct effects on output which have not been correctly modelled. One is left with a concern that the apparent effects of inflation on output, especially since the mid-1970s, are too large to be wholly credible. A related concern is that the methods used to measure both fiscal and monetary policy may have resulted in underestimates of their importance in explaining output movements during the last decade.

Subject to these limitations, we are now in a position to answer the questions addressed by this part of the book. We conclude that it *is* possible to provide a framework within which both the stop-go cycle of the 1960s and the more irregular and violent fluctuations of the 1970s can be explained. That explanation does include an element of systematic periodicity but it is not as important as one might judge from the regularity of turning points in many economic indicators. Output interacts with interest rates and the rate of inflation in a way which probably does tend to perpetuate cyclical fluctuations, but especially in the 1970s much of the fluctuation we experienced was the result of events external to our economy.

7

SUMMARY AND DISCUSSION OF RESULTS

Trade-cycle behaviour, or business-cycle behaviour as Americans call it, consists of fluctuations in the level of economic activity from year to year associated with fluctuations in aggregate demand. It can be observed in most market economies for most periods when appropriate statistics have been collected. Relatively short-term movements of this kind have been very extensively studied by econometricians and model-builders in many countries for many years. It is, in the nature of things, much easier to apply statistical analysis to short-term cyclical movements than to the determination of longer-term trends. It is not surprising therefore that our knowledge of the typical patterns of trade-cycle behaviour is *relatively* complete and *relatively* secure.

We know from repeated experience which variables tend to lead and which tend to lag over the typical trade cycle, which are pro-cyclical and which are counter-cyclical. Knowledge of this kind has been incorporated into macroeconomic models, large and small, and it is used to produce forecasts of economic activity a year or two ahead. Such forecasting, although it is subject to a wide margin of error, can be shown by statistical analysis of outturns and forecasts to contain useful if incomplete information. This study is thus concerned with a subject area that is already well worked over, but its focus is on one aspect of trade-cycle behaviour which has been strangely neglected in recent years.

Periodicity is a tendency for the time elapsed between corresponding phases of successive cycles to be relatively constant. Inspection by eye of British data from 1959 to 1982 suggests periodicity with a cycle length of about four to six years. It is strange therefore that periodicity has been so neglected a subject by British economists since the early 1960s. Economists writing before the early 1960s, although they did not have much recent experience of regular periodicity to draw on, nevertheless sometimes wrote about periodicity as if it were self-evidently a characteristic of trade cycles.

The neglect of periodicity by economists in recent years does not have much to do with the development of macroeconomic theory since the 1960s. It is true that the post-Keynesian multiplier–accelerator models once used to explain the trade cycle have been challenged, but neo-classical or 'new classical' rational expectations models would also allow of periodicity as a possible characteristic of trade-cycle variation. The neglect of the subject stems from the view that periodicity does not in fact occur.

This view is in marked contrast with the actual appearance of the British data. Its tacit acceptance by British economists may be a measure of the extent that we have allowed ourselves to view the world through American eyes. British experience since about 1960 is more periodic than American experience although that does not mean that there is no trace at all of periodicity even in American data, especially in the 1970s. In seeking an explanation of periodicity in this country, therefore, we would expect to find a mechanism at work which is not without parallels anywhere else in the world, or in other eras, but nevertheless something which has been especially active in this country in recent times.

Periodicity is not a hypothesis and we have not attempted to test it. It is a characteristic of trade cycles which one would expect *a priori* to be evident to a greater or lesser degree in different countries and different times. The view expressed by some writers that it does not in fact occur may be the result of an inappropriate statement of the alternatives. The burden of proof has been wrongly placed on those who would argue that trade cycles can be periodic. It would be more appropriate to place that burden on those who would argue that trade cycles *cannot* be periodic, since that would be a theoretical novelty.

The aim of this study is to explain why the trade cycle in Britain from the late 1950s to the early 1980s shows such regular periodicity. This does not mean, however, that it prejudges the issue whether that periodicity is systematic or accidental. If, for example, it could be shown that the cycles of the 1970s were caused by a totally different mechanism to that which produced the cycles of the 1960s, that would be rather good evidence that the impression of a roughly constant cycle length across the two decades was the result of chance, not the result of a tendency to regular periodicity. As we have seen, there is indeed some support for a partial explanation of the periodicity observed along these lines.

Periodicity has been measured in a variety of ways. It is possible that something of interest has been learned in the process about some of the techniques of measurement used, although that has not been the main purpose of the study. All the statistical exercises reported are handi-capped by the short run of data available. Even two and a half decades of relatively uninterrupted, and well documented, experience is not really enough to answer questions about a cycle which roughly repeats itself about every five years. But, of course, this limitation on statistical degrees of freedom is one which this study shares with most other studies in time-series econometrics, many of which are far more ambitious in their aims, and far less qualified than this one in the conclusions they draw.

Several hypotheses about the origin of periodicity can be rejected with fair confidence. Events in this country tend in many ways to mirror events in the world at large. Our economic growth rate, for example, slowed down in the 1970s, and output in this country was adversely affected by two abrupt rises in the price of oil. Our exports depend on world trade. Despite this our trade cycle is not simply a reflection of a world trade cycle and the periodicity we observe in British data is not simply the consequence of periodicity abroad.

Again, changes in fiscal policy have on occasion had a quite powerful effect on the level of economic activity in this country. Measuring these effects raises problems both of definition and data, but we have found no support for the view that the periodicity in the British trade cycle is the product, whether by accident or design, of discretionary budgetary policy. If we were concerned with the 1960s alone the case might be less clearcut, but if we are seeking a consistent explanation of the twenty-five years under review then fiscal policy, even in combination with other factors, can almost certainly be excluded.

Another possible explanation considered but rejected, is the interaction of output growth with the wish of firms to maintain a constant stock-output ratio. It would be to go too far to say that stocks play no role in the mechanism that generates periodicity. But the balance of the evidence seems to be against giving them the dominant role attributed to them in some pre- or immediately postwar writing on the trade cycle.

A Marxian model of fluctuations in the growth of 'capitalist' economies would seem on theoretical grounds better designed to explain variations in the growth of productive potential than the variations in the utilisation of capacity typical of trade cycles. We have not tested models of this kind in this study, partly because of the known deficiencies of data in the capital stock.

We can, however, eliminate a related hypothesis which would attribute periodicity to an interaction between output and labour cost competitiveness. Competitiveness has a powerful effect on output, but it is not itself a cyclical variable. Its influence was felt most powerfully after the exceptional appreciation in sterling at the end of the 1970s, when it certainly contributed to the abrupt cyclical downturn. But for much of the period considered competitiveness hardly changed. It would be very difficult to ascribe much of an explanation of periodicity spanning the 1960s and the 1970s to any mechanism which changed when the fixed exchange rate system was replaced by a relatively free float.

It would not appear that the upper turning points of the cycle in activity each corresponded to some 'ceiling' level of capacity utilisation.

This argues against any model of the trade cycle which is 'explosive' at normal levels of capacity use but kept within limits by 'buffers' of some kind. Models of this kind have not been very thoroughly tested but such evidence as there is tells against them.

These are the negative conclusions; the positive ones must be stated with even more caution. Interest rate movements do seem to have a fairly regular cyclical pattern (and are used for that reason by the CSO in compiling their leading indicators). Their interaction with output may play a significant role in the periodicity observed, although it does not on its own provide an adequate explanation. The nature of that interaction is somewhat obscure. Interest rates tend to rise in the upswing of the cycle, but it would be difficult – impossible even – to say to what extent that reflects conscious policy choices by the monetary authorities, to what extent market forces. Higher interest rates do tend to be followed by a downturn in output but again the mechanism is unclear.

Per percentage point the effect of higher interest rates seemed to be more powerful in the 1960s than in the 1970s, but this may simply indicate that the relationship is not a linear one. Moreover, it seems to be *nominal* interest rates rather than *real* interest rates which contribute to periodicity. There is nothing novel about an emphasis on nominal rather than real rates in empirical observation of trade cycle behaviour, but its basis in theory remains somewhat unsatisfactory.

The rate of inflation seems more important than the rate of interest, especially in the 1970s when it varied much more. Again the theoretical reasons why inflation should reduce output are not as well documented as the fact that it does. Estimating the effect of output on inflation, however, is difficult in the extreme, especially given the successive phases of prices and incomes policy in force during the data period. It seems likely that the periodicity we observe is partly due to the effects of world inflation on inflation in this country, and hence on output. This mechanism, if it occurs, would not be truly systematic since world inflation has been very strongly influenced by two large discrete jumps in the price of oil.

Doubt must remain therefore as to the extent that the periodicity observed in British data is systematic and home-produced, to what extent accidental and imported. It is also doubtful to what extent that periodicity occurred only because of a particular 'regime' in the determination of interest rates, or for that matter because prices and incomes policies were intermittently imposed. A better explanation of the variations in inflation might help resolve these questions. For the present it seems best to conclude that there was, and probably still is, some inherent tendency to periodicity in the British economy but that the special circumstances of the 1970s exaggerated it. The gap between the two oil price shocks happened by coincidence to be rather similar to the time period of a single complete cycle in the British economy.

If the trade cycle were to become more closely synchronised across countries and if oil and other commodity prices are sensitive to cyclical variations in the level of world activity, then events like oil price shocks could themselves come to be systematic and help to transmit what might be a more violent world trade cycle. The closer integration of trade and capital flows must make such an outcome more likely.

If periodicity is interpreted this way, what are the implications for policy analysis and for forecasting? The macroeconomic models used at the National Institute and elsewhere for these two tasks do not explain periodicity or even acknowledge its existence to the extent we have found it in the data series from which they are estimated. Some of the statistical work reported here may have implications for modelbuilding, but the explanation offered of periodicity does not imply that the macroeconomic models are misspecified in any obvious way. They do not attempt to explain policy and they treat the level of interest rates as exogenous, outside the range of variables they are intended to explain. Variation in the world rate of inflation is unquestionably exogenous to the United Kingdom economy. The macroeconomic models could not therefore be expected to explain periodicity in full if it is in fact the result of interactions of the kind described in this paper. Nevertheless, it might be productive to compare the interactions between output and inflation suggested by large macroeconomic models with those suggested by the much simpler approach adopted here.

A proper understanding of periodicity would be essential if the monetary and fiscal authorities were to adopt a 'counter-cyclical' policy and try to smooth out the fluctuations in output. Nothing in this study, however, has suggested that they should do so. Cycles, whether more or less periodic, may be good for the economy. A rational controller of the economy might choose a periodic path. That is not to say, of course, that the fiscal and monetary authorities should not take steps to reverse long-run stagnation or adverse trends in unemployment. It cannot be emphasised too much that the levels and duration of unemployment experienced in the 1930s and again since 1979 are not the result of normal, or benign, trade-cycle variation.

If the aim of policy is not to iron out the cycle it might well be to make it more predictable. As we have seen, the behaviour of the monetary authorities in setting interest rates may well have an important effect on the character of the cycle. If they change their behaviour, as they have done repeatedly in the last few years, they make forecasting the trade cycle more difficult, perhaps for decades ahead.

Any improvement in understanding of trade-cycle behaviour should make forecasting better and in that respect a correct interpretation of periodicity would be no exception. But one must guard against the view that periodicity provides some special esoteric knowledge which changes the nature of forecasting, making it a fundamentally easier task. It would be extremely unwise to extrapolate the periodic pattern of the 1960s and 1970s as if it were a deterministic sine wave. The trade cycle is quite fundamentally different from the cycle of the seasons or the phases of the moon!

Since the upturn of 1981 there have been more than four years of uninterrupted growth (if allowance is made for the miners' strike). Already it seems that the cyclical pattern is changing. The upswing, although too weak to cut unemployment significantly, has increased the index of capacity utilisation and the level of unfilled vacancies. Although not a strong upswing it has been sustained.

Periodicity is not so regular or so systematic that the end of this upswing can be confidently predicted. All we can do is to point to the kind of circumstances likely to bring it to an end. If there were a recession abroad that would obviously tend to pull down the British economy as well. If nominal interest rates were to rise, as they did for example early in 1985, that might signal the approach of a downturn. If inflation were to accelerate, or even perhaps if it were just to stop falling, that would be another warning of an approaching peak.

The trade cycle has always been accompanied by an even more marked cycle in the mood of commentators on the economy. In the downswing there is talk of secular stagnation, in the upswing of economic miracles. One reason for studying the trade cycle is to try to distinguish cycle from trend. One can predict with some confidence that cyclical fluctuations will continue. But, even though the cycles may be to a degree periodic, that does not mean that one can say when they will occur.

NOTES

NOTES TO CHAPTER 1

1 The cyclical indicators are published monthly in *Economic Trends*. Their compilation is described in articles in that periodical in March 1975, May 1976 and May 1980. The work done at the CSO builds on a study at the National Institute, reported in O'Dea (1975).
2 Except interpolation. See *Economic Trends*, May 1976, p. 68.
3 As an example of this usage, and a useful source for recent developments in the theory of the trade cycle, see Barro (1981) in which, despite its title, periodicity is never mentioned.
4 No attempt will be made to review this literature, which is surveyed in Zarnowitz (1985). An excellent starting point for readers unfamiliar with trade-cycle theory as it was taught in the 1950s–1960s would be Matthews (1959), Baumol (1959) or Allen (1959) especially chapters 7 to 9. To get an idea of the issues which were seen as central at the beginning of the 1940s see Davies (1941) especially Chapters 8 and 12.

NOTES TO CHAPTER 2

1 For trade-cycle theory up to the late 1950s the necessary mathematics is set out in Allen (1959). For the mathematics used in more recent contributions the best reference is probably Sargent (1979).
2 Amongst the best known examples of non-linear models are those described in Goodwin (1951), Hicks (1950) and Kalecki (1935). For recent work in this tradition see Goodwin, Krüger and Vercelli (1984).
3 One must beware, however, of dismissing the non-linear alternative too easily. Blatt (1978) demonstrates how well a linear stochastic model seems to 'explain' artificial data generated by a non-linear model constructed for the purpose. The issue is taken up again in Chapter 4 where a method of distinguishing between linear and non-linear models is proposed.
4 The use of the linear stochastic model to explain the trade cycle dates back to Frisch (1933).
5 The formula and its derivation is given in Kendall (1946), one of the earliest of the National Institute's Occasional Papers.
6 For this and many related points discussed in this study see Harvey (1981) or Kendall and Stuart (1975).
7 The classical study is Volterra (1931). An interesting study of biological data by econometricians, especially relevant to periodicity in the trade cycle is Chan and Wallis (1978).

8 The difference between the cyclical behaviour possible in large models and small models is discussed in Klein (1983). In this he cites Otsuki (1971) which is concerned with the particular case of multiple roots or, more generally, roots that are unevenly distributed over the range of possible values.

NOTES TO CHAPTER 3

1 The reasons given for persistence include: adjustment costs, in Sargent (1979), inventory accumulation, in Blinder and Fischer (1981) and wage contracts, in Taylor (1980).
2 For a brief description of monetarist models of the business cycle and a criticism of their empirical validity, see Sims (1983).
3 The literature on the 'political business cycle' derives from Nordhaus (1975) which is still probably the most relevant reference for this study.
4 The ground is very well covered in Sargent (1979). The application of the 'rational expectations hypothesis' to output as well as to prices is now well established in the literature. It is being applied increasingly to models which are Keynesian in origin, which allow for market disequilibrium and which are based on imperfect rather than perfect competition. See Begg (1982) and also for practical applications, recent National Institute discussion papers, including Hall *et al.* (1984).
5 See especially Phillips (1954) and Phillips (1957) but also the discussion of the British experience in Bronfenbrenner (1969).
6 The earliest reference is Adelman and Adelman (1959). Several important studies are reported in Hickman (1972).
7 The account of the DRI model in Kelley (1978) is one exception. Another exception is the model of the British economy used by the Treasury in 1982. Its structure and its simulation properties are described in HMT (1982). In this last case periodicity can be traced to the specification of the earnings equation, which produces a cyclical response in real earnings to a change in the level of output. The equation has since been changed and the simulation results no longer show periodicity of a significant kind.
8 In Adelman and Adelman (1959) the length of the cycle in their artificial data is estimated by counting the gaps between turning points. On this basis it is reported that the average cycle lasts four years, which was thought to be similar to that found in American business cycle data. However, the model used was an annual one. If the odds are fifty-fifty that each observation is a turning point, then the average full cycle measured this way will always be four time periods. Perhaps this finding of the Adelman and Adelman study has therefore been given more attention than it deserves. In the present context it is also important to note that the distribution of cycle lengths recorded for their simulation results is not such as to indicate periodicity at all.
9 The statistical problems of distinguishing between these models are discussed in Nelson and Plosser (1982).

1 'Because business fluctuations are so irregular it is perhaps surprising that they are called 'cycles'', Wonnacott and Wonnacott (1982).
2 'Since most economic time series do not display pronounced peaks in their spectrum at the business-cycle frequencies, it is probably correct to say that such a condition is not a key feature of the business cycle', Long and Plosser (1983).
3 In Matthews (1959) it is shown that the behaviour of fixed investment is different in different cycles.
4 The programme used is described in Osborn (1977). The addition of a third-order term on the left-hand side of the equation is, in the case of a univariate model, equivalent to the introduction of a first-order autoregressive error model on the right-hand side. The moving-average error programme in four of the six cases produced a result at, or close to, the boundary condition for invertibility. This suggests that better results could be obtained by transforming the data before estimation.
5 This interpretation of periodicity contrasts with that adopted in McCulloch (1975) where periodicity is 'tested', using mainly American data, with mixed results.
6 The term to 'encompass' is used in this sense in Mizon (1984).

1 'To produce a continuous indicator series the available values are taken from the survey months and the intervening months are obtained by interpolation', *Economic Trends*, May 1976, p. 68.
2 If the aim of this study were to provide the best estimate of the effects of fiscal policy on the economy – which it is not – then it would be appropriate to estimate the equations in which current value of the policy index occurs using the technique of 'instrumental variables'.

REFERENCES

Adelman, I. and Adelman, F. L., 'The dynamic properties of the Klein-Goldberger model', *Econometrica*, vol. 27(4), October 1959, pp. 596–625.

Allen, R. G. D., *Mathematical Economics*, 2nd edition, Macmillan, 1959.

Artis, M. *et al.*, 'The effects of economic policy', *National Institute Economic Review*, no. 108, May 1984.

Barro, R. J. (Ed.), *Money, Expectations and Business Cycles*, NY, Academic Press, 1981.

Baumol, W. J., *Economic Dynamics*, 2nd edition, Macmillan, 1970.

Begg, D. K. H., *The Rational Expectations Revolution in Macroeconomics: Theories and Evidence*, Baltimore, Johns Hopkins University Press, 1982.

Blatt, J. M., 'On the econometric approach to business-cycle analysis', *Oxford Economic Papers*, 30, July 1978, pp. 292–300.

Blinder, A. S. and Fischer, S., 'Inventories, rational expectations and the business cycle', *Journal of Monetary Economics*, vol. 8(3), November 1981, pp. 277–304.

Bronfenbrenner, M., *Is the Business Cycle Obsolete?*, NY, John Wiley & Sons, 1969.

Chan, W.-Y. T. and Wallis, K. F., 'Multiple time series modelling: another look at the mink-muskrat interaction', *Applied Statistics*, vol. 27, no. 2, 1978, pp. 168–75.

Darby, J., 'Fiscal policy and interest rates', *National Institute Economic Review*, no. 109, August 1984.

Davies, H. T., *The Analysis of Economic Time Series*, Cowles Commission, 1941.

Fishman, G. S., *Spectral Methods in Econometrics*, Harvard University Press, 1970.

Frisch, R., 'Propagation problems and impulse problems in dynamic economics' in *Economic Essays in Honour of Gustav Cassel*, London, George Allen and Unwin, 1933.

Goodwin, R. M., 'The non-linear accelerator and the persistence of business cycles', *Econometrica*, vol. 19(1), January 1951, pp. 1–17.

Goodwin, R. M., Krüger, M. and Vercelli, A. (Eds), *Non-linear Models of Fluctuating Growth*, Springer-Verlag, 1984.

Gordon, R. J., 'Output fluctuations and gradual price adjustment', *Journal of Economic Literature*, vol. 19(2), June 1981, pp. 493–530.

Granger, C. W. J., 'The typical spectral shape of an economic variable', *Econometrica*, vol. 34(1), January 1966, pp. 150–61.

Hall, S. G., Henry, S. G. B. and Wren-Lewis, S., 'Manufacturing stocks and forward looking expectations in the UK', National Institute of Economic and Social Research Discussion Paper no. 64, 1984.

Harvey, A. C., *Time Series Models*, Phillip Allan, 1981.

'Trends and cycles in macroeconomic time series', *Journal of Business and Economic Statistics*, vol. 3, 216–27, 1985.

Henry, S. G. B. and Johns, C. H., 'Simulations on NIESR Model 7', National Institute of Economic and Social Research, mimeo, 1985.

Hicks, J. R., *A Contribution to the Theory of the Trade Cycle*, Oxford, Clarendon Press, 1950.

Hickman, B. G. (Ed.), *Econometric Models of Cyclical Behavior*, NY, Columbia University Press for NBER, 1972.

Kalecki, M., 'A macroeconomic theory of business cycles', *Econometrica*, vol. 3, 1935, pp. 327–44.

Kelley, J., 'The American business cycle' in 'Evidence from the DRI model', *Data Resources Review*, September 1978, pp. 9–23.

Kendall, M. G., *Contributions to the Study of Oscillatory Time-Series*, Cambridge University Press, 1946.

Kendall, M. G. and Stuart, A., *The Advanced Theory of Statistics*, vol. 3, *Design and Analysis, and Time-series*, 3rd edition, Griffin, 1976.

Keynes, J. M., *General Theory of Employment, Interest and Money*, London, Macmillan, 1936, chapter 22, Notes on the Trade Cycle.

Klein, L. R. and Welfe, W. (Eds), *Lectures in Econometrics*, Elsevier, 1983, chapter 4.

Long, J. B. and Plosser, C. I., 'Real business cycles', *Journal of Political Economy*, vol. 91(1), February 1983, pp. 39–69.

Matthews, R. C. O., *The Trade Cycle*, Cambridge University Press, 1959.

McCulloch, J. H., 'The Monte Carlo cycle in business activity', *Economic Inquiry*, vol. 13(3), September 1975, pp. 303–21.

Mitchell, W. C., *Business Cycles: The Problem and its Setting*, NY, NBER, 1927, p. 468.

Mizon, G. E., 'The encompassing approach in econometrics' in Hendry and Wallis (Eds), *Econometrics and Quantitative Economics*, Blackwell, 1984.

Nelson, C. R. and Plosser, C. I., 'Trends and random walks in macroeconomic time series: some evidence and implications', *Journal of Monetary Economics*, vol. 10(2), September 1982, pp. 139–62.

Nordhaus, W. D., 'The political business cycle', *Review of Economic Studies*, vol. 42(2), April 1975, pp. 169–90.

O'Dea, D. J., *Cyclical Indicators for the Post-War British Economy*, Cambridge University Press, 1975.

Osborn, D.. R., 'Exact and approximate likelihood estimators for vector moving average processes', *Journal of the Royal Statistical Society*, Series B, vol. 39(1), 1977, pp. 114–8.

Otsuki, M., 'Oscillations in stochastic simulation of linear systems', *Economic Studies Quarterly*, vol. 22(3), December 1971, pp. 54–71.

Phillips, A. W., 'Stabilisation policy in a closed economy', *Economic Journal*, vol. 64, no. 254, June 1954, pp. 290–323.

'Stabilisation policy and the time-forms of lagged responses', *Economic Journal*, vol. 67, no. 266, June 1957, pp. 265–77.

Salmon, M., 'Error correction mechanisms', *Economic Journal*, vol. 92, no. 367, September 1982, p. 615.

Sargent, T. J., *Macroeconomic Theory*, NY, Academic Press, 1979.

Sims, C. A., 'Is there a monetary business cycle?', *American Economic Review*, vol. 73(2), May 1983, pp. 228–33.

Volterra, V., *Leçons sur la Théorie Mathématique de la Lutte pour la Vie*, Gautier-Villars, 1931.

Wallis, K. F., 'Multiple time series analysis and the final form of econometric models', *Econometrica*, vol. 45, no. 6, September 1977, pp. 1481–1497.

Wonnacott, P. and Wonnacott, R. J., *Economics*, 2nd edition, McGraw-Hill, 1982, p. 326.

Wren-Lewis, S., 'The role of output expectations and liquidity in explaining recent productivity movements', *National Institute Economic Review* no. 108, May 1984.

Zarnowitz, V., 'Recent work on business cycles in historical perspective', *Journal of Economic Literature*, vol. XXIII, no. 2, June 1985, pp. 523–80.

INDEX

Adelman, F. L., 90
Adelman, I., 90
aggregation, 22, 24
Allen, R. G. D., 89
Artis, M., 65

Barro, R. J., 89
Baumol, W. J., 89
Begg, D. K. H., 90
biological cycles, 10, 11
Blatt, J. M., 37, 51, 89
Blinder, A. S., 90
Bronfenbrenner, M., 90
business cycles, *see* trade cycles

Central Statistical Office (CSO), 2, 46, 48, 50,
    52, 60–2, 64, 85, 89
Chan, W.-Y. T., 89
Confederation of British Industry (CBI), 2, 52,
    61–2, 65

Darby, J., 72
Davies, H. T., 89

Fischer, S., 90
Fishman, G. S., 48
forecasting, 86
Frisch, R., 89

Goodwin, R. M., 28, 89
Gordon, R. J., 26
Granger, C. W. J., 45

Harvey, A. C., 37, 39, 41, 48, 89
Hickman, B. G., 90
Hicks, J. R., 52, 89
hog cycle, 25

International Monetary Fund (IMF), 64, 67, 80

Kalman filter, 39
Kelley, J., 90
Kendall, M. G., 89
Keynes, J. M., 27
Klein, L. R., 90
Krüger, M., 29, 89

limit cycles, 6, 29, 51–2
Long, J. B., 91
long waves, 12, 37

Matthews, R. C. O., 3, 89, 91
Mizon, G. E., 91

Nelson, C. R., 39, 90
Nordhaus, W. D., 90

O'Dea, D. J., 89
Osborn, D. R., 91
Otsuki, M., 90

periodicity, 1–3
    and rational expectations, 13–15, 22, 24, 25,
        28, 35
    effects of government policy on, 16–18, 21, 27,
        56, 61–6, 84
    effects of world economy on, 18, 35, 56, 66,
        78–81, 84, 85
    in America, 1–3, 16, 17, 31, 42–5, 83
    in trade-cycle theory, ch. 3, 36, 82
    mathematics of, 3, ch. 2, 18–21, 25–6
    measurement of, 36–9, 83
        in quarterly indicator series, 46–8
        in unemployment, 39–45
    without control, 21–4
persistence, in trade cycle, 2, 16, 70
Phillips, A. W., 66, 90
Plosser, C. I., 39, 90, 91
political business cycle theory, 17
prey and predators, 10, 11

quarterly data, 45

Salmon, M., 21
Sargent, T. J., 45, 89, 90
Savage, D., 68
seasonality, 14–15, 17, 28, 55
Sims, C. A., 90
Stuart, A., 89
sunspots, 16

temperature, data in, 55

trade cycle behaviour,
   interaction of variables in, 9–12, 13, 30, 35,
      47, 54–9, 66–9, 77
trade cycle theory, 3, 12
trade cycles,
   as distinct from trends, 33–4, 38–9, 67, 87
   causes of, 16–18, 21, 27
   history of, ch. 6
   length of, 2, 36 (see also persistence)
   models of,
      behavioural, 53, 54, 66
      Keynesian, 27–8, 29, 90
      large macroeconomic, 30, 31–3
      Marxian, 28–9, 84
      role of stock cycles in, 76–7, 84
   variability of, 2 (see also periodicity)
trends, 48
   in level of output, 33–4

   in level of unemployment, 33, 34, 42
   in price level, 33

unemployment, periodicity of,
   in GDP, 49–50
   in United Kingdom, 41–5, 48–50
   in United States, 42–5

Vercelli, A., 28, 89
Volterra, V., 89

Wallis, K. F., 37, 89
Wonnacott, P., 91
Wonnacott, R. J., 91
Wren-Lewis, S., 65

Zarnowitz, V., 3, 89

THE NATIONAL INSTITUTE OF ECONOMIC
AND SOCIAL RESEARCH
PUBLICATIONS IN PRINT

published by
THE CAMBRIDGE UNIVERSITY PRESS
(available from booksellers, or in case of difficulty from the publishers)

ECONOMIC AND SOCIAL STUDIES

XIX   *The Antitrust Laws of the USA: A Study of Competition Enforced by Law*
   by A. D. NEALE and D. G. GOYDER. 3rd edn, 1980. pp. 548. £37.50 net.

XXI   *Industrial Growth and World Trade: An Empirical Study of Trends in Production, Consumption and Trade in Manufactures from 1899–1959 with a Discussion of Probable Future Trends*
   By ALFRED MAIZELS. Reprinted with corrections, 1971. pp. 563. £22.50 net.

XXV   *Exports and Economic Growth of Developing Countries*
   By ALFRED MAIZELS assisted by L. F. CAMPBELL-BOROSS and P. B. W. RAYMENT. 1968. pp. 445. £20.00 net.

XXVI   *Urban Development in Britain: Standards, Costs and Resources, 1964–2004*
   By P. A. STONE. Vol I: *Population Trends and Housing*. 1970. pp. 436. £22.50 net.

XXVII   *The Framework of Regional Economics in the United Kingdom*
   By A. J. BROWN. 1972. pp. 372. £22.50 net.

XXVIII   *The Structure, Size and Costs of Urban Settlements*
   By P. A. STONE. 1973. pp. 304. £18.50 net.

XXIX   *The Diffusion of New Industrial Processes: An International Study*
   Edited by L. NABSETH and G. F. RAY. 1974. pp. 346. £22.50 net.

XXXI   *British Economic Policy, 1960–74*
   Edited by F. T. BLACKABY. 1978. pp. 710. £40.00 net.

XXXII   *Industrialisation and the Basis for Trade*
   By R. A. BATCHELOR, R. L. MAJOR and A. D. MORGAN. 1980. pp. 380. £27.50 net.

XXXIII   *Productivity and Industrial Structure*
   By S. J. PRAIS. 1982. pp. 410. £27.50 net.

XXXIV   *World Inflation since 1950. An International Comparative Study*
   By A. J. BROWN assisted by JANE DARBY. 1985. pp. 428. £27.50 net.

OCCASIONAL PAPERS

XXIX   *Poverty and Progress in Britain, 1953–73*
   By G. C. FIEGEHEN, P. S. LANSLEY and A. D. SMITH. 1977. pp. 192. £12.95 net.

XXXI   *Diversification and Competition*
   By M. A. UTTON. 1979. pp. 124. £10.50 net.

XXXII   *Concentration in British Industry, 1935–75*
   By P. E. HART and R. CLARKE. 1980. pp. 178. £13.50 net.

XXXIII   *State Pensions in Britain*
   By J. CREEDY. 1982. pp. 112. £12.50 net.

XXXIV   *International Industrial Productivity*
   By A. D. SMITH, D. M. W. N. HITCHENS and S. W. DAVIES. 1982. pp. 184. £17.50 net.

XXXV   *Concentration and Foreign Trade*
   By M. A. UTTON and A. D. MORGAN. 1983. pp. 150. £17.50 net.

XXXVI   *The Diffusion of Mature Technologies*
   By GEORGE F. RAY. 1984. pp. 96. £15.00 net.

XXXVII   *Productivity in the Distributive Trades. A Comparison of Britain, America and Germany*
   By A. D. SMITH and D. M. W. N. HITCHENS. 1985. pp. 160. £17.50 net.

Publications in Print

XXXVIII   *Profits and Stability of Monopoly*
By M. A. UTTON. 1986. pp. 102. About £15.00 net.

NIESR STUDENTS EDITION
2. *The Antitrust Laws of the U.S.A.* (3rd edition, unabridged)
By A. D. NEALE and D. G. GOYDER. 1980. pp. 548. £12.50 net.
4. *British Economic Policy, 1960–74: Demand Management* (an abridged version of *British Economic Policy, 1960–74*)
Edited by F. T. BLACKABY. 1979. pp. 472. £11.95 net.
5. *The Evolution of Giant Firms in Britain* (2nd impression with a new preface)
By S. J. PRAIS. 1981. pp. 344. £9.95 net.

THE NATIONAL INSTITUTE OF ECONOMIC AND SOCIAL RESEARCH

publishes regularly

THE NATIONAL INSTITUTE ECONOMIC REVIEW

A quarterly analysis of the general economic situation in the United Kingdom and overseas, with forecasts eighteen months ahead. The last issue each year usually contains an assessment of medium-term prospects. There are also in most issues special articles on subjects of interest to academic and business economists.

Annual subscriptions, £45.00 (home), and £60.00 (abroad), also single issues for the current year, £12.50 (home) and £18.00 (abroad), are available direct from NIESR, 2 Dean Trench Street, Smith Square, London, SW1P 3EH.

Subscriptions at the special reduced price of £18.00 p.a. are available to students in the United Kingdom and Irish Republic on application to the Secretary of the Institute.

Back numbers and reprints of issues which have gone out of stock are distributed by Wm. Dawson and Sons Ltd., Cannon House, Park Farm Road, Folkestone. Microfiche copies for the years 1959–84 are available from E P Microform Ltd., Bradford Road, East Ardsley, Wakefield, Yorks.

Published by
HEINEMANN EDUCATIONAL BOOKS
(distributed by Gower Publishing Company and available from booksellers)

THE UNITED KINGDOM ECONOMY
By the NIESR. 5th edition, 1982. pp. 119. £2.25 net.
DEMAND MANAGEMENT
Edited by MICHAEL POSNER. 1978. pp. 256. £6.95 net.
DE-INDUSTRIALISATION
Edited by FRANK BLACKABY. 1979. pp. 282. £6.96 (paperback) net.
BRITAIN IN EUROPE
Edited by WILLIAM WALLACE. 1980. pp. 224. £6.50 (paperback) net.
THE FUTURE OF PAY BARGAINING
Edited by FRANK BLACKABY. 1980. pp. 256. £16.00 (hardback), £6.50 (paperback) net.
INDUSTRIAL POLICY AND INNOVATION
Edited by CHARLES CARTER. 1981. pp. 250. £16.00 (hardback), £6.95 (paperback) net.
THE CONSTITUTION OF NORTHERN IRELAND
Edited by DAVID WATT. 1981. pp. 233. £15.00 (hardback), £7.50 (paperback) net.

Publications in Print

RETIREMENT POLICY. THE NEXT FIFTY YEARS
Edited by MICHAEL FOGARTY. 1982. pp. 224. £15.00 (hardback), £6.95 (paperback) net.

SLOWER GROWTH IN THE WESTERN WORLD
Edited by R. C. O. MATTHEWS. 1982. pp. 182. £17.50 (hardback), £6.95 (paperback) net.

NATIONAL INTERESTS AND LOCAL GOVERNMENT
Edited by KEN YOUNG. 1983. pp. 180. £15.00 (hardback), £8.95 (paperback) net.

EMPLOYMENT OUTPUT AND INFLATION
Edited by A. J. C. BRITTON. 1983. pp. 208. £21.00 net.

THE TROUBLED ALLIANCE. ATLANTIC RELATIONS IN THE 1980s
Edited by LAWRENCE FREEDMAN. 1983. pp. 176. £16.50 (hardback), £6.50 (paperback) net.

EDUCATION AND ECONOMIC PERFORMANCE
Edited by G. D. N. WORSWICK. 1984. pp. 152. £16.50 net.

Published by
GOWER PUBLISHING COMPANY LTD

ENERGY SELF-SUFFICIENCY FOR THE UK
Edited by ROBERT BELGRAVE and MARGARET CORNELL. 1985. pp. 224. £19.50 net.

THE FUTURE OF BRITISH DEFENCE POLICY
Edited by JOHN ROPER. 1985. pp. 214. £18.50 net.

ENERGY MANAGEMENT: CAN WE LEARN FROM OTHERS?
By GEORGE F. RAY. 1985. pp. 131. £18.50 net

UNEMPLOYMENT AND LABOUR MARKET POLICIES
Edited by P. E. HART. 1986. pp. 230. About £18.50 net.